WHAT IS THE BOOK OF ACTS?

Kids' Guides to God's Word Series

What Is the Book of

ACTS?

Michael Whitworth

ISBN 978-1-971767-38-3

Published by Start2Finish
Bend, Oregon 97702
start2finish.org

Printed in the United States of America
30 29 28 27 26   1 2 3 4 5

For Mary and Heather, my beloved cousins—

*whose love for that old Jerusalem gospel and its messengers
has carried this series from the beginning.*

*Your support for these books has been enormous,
and the truth is simple: the Kids' Guides to God's Word
series wouldn't exist without you.*

With gratitude and love.

CONTENTS

INTRODUCTION

Picture this: your coach has been running every practice, calling every play, and winning every game. The team depends on him completely. Then one day he walks into the locker room and says, "I'm leaving. The mission is yours now. Go win the championship." And before anyone can ask a question, he's gone.

That's essentially what happened at the beginning of the book of Acts. Jesus had spent three years teaching his followers, performing miracles, and demonstrating what the kingdom of God looked like up close. Then he rose from the dead, spent forty more days preparing them, and ascended into heaven. The mission to reach the entire world now belonged to a small group of ordinary men and women huddled together in an upper room in Jerusalem.

They had no money. No political connections. No buildings, no organization, no strategy beyond a single command and a single promise. The command: be my witnesses to the ends of the earth. The promise: you will receive power when the Holy Spirit comes on you.

That's it. That's what they had. And within a single generation, the message of Jesus spread from a rented room in Jerusalem to the heart of the Roman Empire.

The book of Acts is the story of how it happened.

WHERE WE ARE IN THE STORY

Acts was written by Luke, the same man who wrote the Gospel that bears his name. Luke was a physician, a Gentile, and a careful historian who traveled with the apostle Paul on several missionary journeys. His Gospel told the story of what Jesus did and taught from his birth through his resurrection. Acts picks up right where the Gospel left off, which is why some scholars call it "Luke volume two."

But here's the crucial detail. When Luke introduced Acts, he described his Gospel as an account of "all that Jesus began to do and teach." That word "began" changes everything. Luke wasn't saying the story of Jesus was finished. He was saying it was just getting started. The Gospel told what Jesus did in person, walking the roads of Galilee and Judea. Acts tells what Jesus continued to do through his Spirit, working in and through his followers as the gospel moved outward across the known world.

To understand why this moment mattered so much, you need to remember the backstory. God had promised Abraham that through his descendants all nations would be blessed. That promise echoed through the centuries, through Moses and David and the prophets, always pointing forward to someone who would come and set everything right. Jesus was that someone. He lived the life Israel couldn't live, died the death sinners deserved, and rose again to prove that God had accepted his sacrifice. But the rescue mission wasn't finished when Jesus walked out of the tomb. The news still had to reach the world. Someone had to carry it.

That's where Acts begins. The risen King gives his followers their assignment, sends his Spirit to empower them, and the most unlikely revolution in history takes off.

WHAT YOU'RE ABOUT TO READ

Jesus gave his followers a roadmap in Acts 1:8, and Luke used it as the outline for his entire book. "You will be my witnesses in Jerusalem, and in all Judea and Samaria, and to the ends of the earth." If you watch for that pattern, the book's structure falls right into place.

The first section (chapters 1–7) takes place in Jerusalem. The Holy Spirit arrives on the day of Pentecost, Peter preaches and three thousand people respond, the young church grows rapidly, and the religious leaders who killed Jesus begin pushing back hard. This section ends with the stoning of Stephen, the first follower of Jesus to die for his faith. His death seems like a disaster, but it turns out to be the spark that sends the gospel outward.

The middle section (chapters 8–12) follows the gospel as it breaks beyond Jerusalem into Judea and Samaria. You'll meet Philip, who carries the message to people the Jewish establishment would never have accepted. You'll watch the dramatic conversion of Saul, the church's most dangerous enemy, who becomes its most important missionary. And you'll see Peter learn a lesson that shakes everything he thought he knew: God's rescue isn't just for Jewish people. It's for everyone.

The final section (chapters 13–28) follows Paul on three missionary journeys across the Roman Empire. He plants churches in cities you can still visit today. He faces riots, beatings, shipwrecks, and prison cells. He stands before governors and kings and never stops preaching. The book ends with Paul in Rome, the capital of the empire, still proclaiming Jesus to anyone who will listen.

You'll encounter some of the most dramatic scenes in the entire Bible. A room shaken by the Holy Spirit. A man struck blind on a road to Damascus. Prison doors blown open by an earthquake. A shipwreck survived by every soul on board. And sermon after sermon after sermon, because if there's one thing the early Christians never stopped doing, it was talking about Jesus.

WHY THIS BOOK MATTERS

Acts matters because it answers a question you might not realize you're asking: What happened next?

The Gospels tell us who Jesus is. The letters of Paul and the other apostles explain what it means to follow him. But Acts is the bridge between the two. It shows how the message got from a hillside in Galilee to living rooms and marketplaces across the Roman world. Without Acts, there's a gap in the story you can't fill.

But Acts does more than fill a historical gap. It shows us what the church is supposed to look like. The earliest Christians devoted themselves to the apostles' teaching, to fellowship, to breaking bread together, and to prayer. They shared what they had. They cared for the poor. They told the truth even when it cost them everything. They weren't perfect, and Acts doesn't pretend they were. But they were serious about following Jesus, and the world noticed.

Acts also shows us how people became Christians. This might surprise you if you're used to hearing that all you need to do is "accept Jesus into your heart." That phrase never appears in Acts. What you'll find instead is a consistent pattern: people heard the good news about Jesus, believed it, repented of their sins, and were baptized or immersed. Every conversion story in Acts follows this shape. It happened on the day of Pentecost. It happened with the Ethiopian on a desert road. It happened with Saul in Damascus. It happened with Lydia by a river and a jailer in the middle of the night. The Christ who commanded the mission also defined the response.

And Acts matters because it's an honest book. The early church wasn't a group of superheroes floating above the problems of ordinary life. They argued about money. They disagreed about who could be included. Their leaders made mistakes. One of their sharpest conflicts involved two of the greatest men in the movement. Luke doesn't hide any of it. He shows us real people stumbling forward in faith, empowered by the Spirit, making Christ known in a world that didn't always want to hear it.

BEFORE YOU BEGIN

A few things to keep in mind as you read.

Acts moves fast. Luke covers roughly thirty years of history, and he doesn't slow down often. Cities, characters, and crises pile up quickly. Don't worry if you can't keep every name and place straight on the first pass. The big picture is what matters, and the big picture is always the same: the gospel is advancing, and nothing can stop it.

The book has two main human characters: Peter dominates the first half, and Paul dominates the second. But the real main character is the Holy Spirit. Luke mentions the Spirit nearly sixty times. The Spirit empowers the preaching, directs the mission, opens doors, shuts doors, and transforms everyone he touches. Without the Spirit, nothing in Acts happens.

There is also real suffering in this book. People are arrested, beaten, stoned, and killed for following Jesus. The road from Jerusalem to Rome is paved with sacrifice. Acts doesn't romanticize this. It shows us what faithfulness costs, and it shows us that God is worth the price.

Finally, Acts doesn't really end. The last chapter finds Paul in Rome, under house arrest, still preaching the kingdom of God "with all boldness and without hindrance." There's no dramatic conclusion, no final curtain. Luke stops writing, but the story doesn't stop. It keeps going, through the centuries, through Christ's people in every generation, all the way down to you.

The same Spirit who filled that upper room in Jerusalem is still at work. The same gospel Peter preached on Pentecost is still the power of God for salvation. And the same mission Jesus gave his followers is still waiting to be carried forward.

Ready?

Turn the page.

1

THE SEQUEL BEGINS

Have you ever watched a movie and then, right at the end, something happens that makes you realize the story isn't over?

That's exactly what happens at the close of *Back to the Future*. Marty McFly has made it home safely. The adventure seems finished. But then Doc Brown comes screeching into the driveway in a flying DeLorean, tells Marty there's an urgent new mission, and blasts off into the sky. The credits roll, and you know: the real adventure is only getting started.

The book of Acts opens the same way.

Luke, the same man who wrote the Gospel that bears his name, is picking up right where he left off. His first book told the story of what Jesus did and taught during his time on earth. It covered his birth, his miracles, his teaching, his death on the cross, and his resurrection from the dead. But that story, as incredible as it was, was only the beginning. Now Luke has a second volume to write. And it starts with the risen Jesus standing among his followers, giving them a mission that will change the world, and then ascending into the sky and disappearing into a cloud.

The first adventure is over. The next one is about to begin. But the disciples can't start yet. They're missing something.

THE STORY CONTINUES

Luke opens his second book by speaking directly to a man named Theophilus, the same person he had addressed in his Gospel. "I wrote about all that Jesus began to do and teach," Luke says, "until the day he was taken up to heaven" (1:1–2).

Did you catch that word? *Began.* Luke doesn't say he wrote about everything Jesus did, as though the story were wrapped up with a bow. He says he wrote about what Jesus *began* to do. That single word tells you everything about why this second book exists. The story of Jesus didn't end when he ascended into heaven. It continued. And the book of Acts is the record of how it continued, not through Jesus walking the dusty roads of Galilee anymore, but through his apostles, empowered by his Spirit, carrying his message to the ends of the earth.

But before any of that could happen, Jesus had some final preparation to do.

After his resurrection, Jesus didn't disappear immediately. He spent forty days with his apostles, appearing to them, eating with them, and teaching them about the kingdom of God (1:3). Forty days. Think about that. Nearly six weeks of personal, face-to-face instruction from the risen Son of God. Luke tells us that Jesus gave them "many convincing proofs" that he was alive. He wasn't a ghost or a hallucination. He stood among them in a real, physical body. He ate fish with them. He let them see his hands. He walked and talked and taught, and he did it all so that when the time came for them to stand up in front of hostile crowds and declare that Jesus had risen from the dead, they could speak as men who knew it was true because they had seen it with their own eyes.

And what did he teach them during those forty days? The kingdom of God. This was always Jesus' central message. Before his death he preached it constantly, and now, after his resurrection, he returned to the same subject. He was showing his apostles how everything that had happened to him, his suffering, his death, and his rising, fit into God's plan for the world. He was opening their minds to understand the Scriptures in a way they never had before.

WAIT FOR IT

During one of those meals together, Jesus gave his apostles a specific command. Don't leave Jerusalem. Stay there and wait for "the promise of the Father," which he described as being "baptized with the Holy Spirit" (1:4–5). John the Baptist had baptized people in water, Jesus reminded them, but something far greater was coming. The Spirit of God himself was about to come upon them with power they had never experienced.

This must have been frustrating to hear. These men had just spent three years following Jesus. They had watched him die. They had seen him alive again. They were ready to do something. And now he was telling them to sit still and wait.

But waiting was part of the plan. The apostles couldn't carry out their mission on their own strength. They needed power that only God could give them. Without the Holy Spirit, they would be unprepared for the enormous work ahead. The mission was far too big for human effort alone. Before the gospel could go anywhere, the power had to come down.

THE WRONG QUESTION AND THE RIGHT ANSWER

The apostles, though, had something else on their minds. "Lord," they asked, "are you at this time going to restore the kingdom to Israel?" (1:6).

It's an honest question, and you can understand why they asked it. For centuries, the Jewish people had lived under the control of foreign empires. The Babylonians, the Persians, the Greeks, and now the Romans had all ruled over them. The prophets had promised that God would one day restore Israel's glory, that a king from David's line would reign forever. The apostles believed Jesus was that king. And now that he had conquered death itself, surely the time had come for him to throw off the Romans, sit on David's throne, and make everything right.

But they were thinking too small.

Jesus didn't exactly say no to their question. But he completely redirected their thinking. "It is not for you to know the times or dates the Father has set by his own authority," he told them. "But you will receive power when the Holy Spirit comes on you, and you will be my witnesses in Jerusalem, and in all Judea and Samaria, and to the ends of the earth" (1:7–8).

Read that last verse one more time. It's one of the most important sentences in the entire Bible.

The apostles were thinking about political power and national borders. Jesus was thinking about something far bigger. He wasn't interested in overthrowing Rome. He was launching a mission that would reach every corner of the globe. And he was handing that mission to them.

Notice the roadmap. First, Jerusalem. Then the surrounding region of Judea and the neighboring territory of Samaria. And finally, to the ends of the earth. This isn't just a general instruction. It's actually the outline for the entire book of Acts. Chapters 1–7 take place in Jerusalem. Chapters 8–12 move into Judea and Samaria. And from chapter 13 to the end, the gospel spreads outward across the Roman Empire, all the way to the capital city of Rome itself.

Jesus wasn't being vague about what he wanted. He was giving them a map. And the commission he had given them before, to go into all the world and preach the gospel to every creature, immersing those who believed, was the key to the entire journey that lay ahead. Everything the apostles would do in the coming years would flow from these marching orders.

INTO THE CLOUD

After saying these things, something happened that none of them could have expected. "He was taken up before their very eyes, and a cloud hid him from their sight" (1:9).

Try to picture this moment. The man they had followed for three years, the one they had watched die on a cross, the one they had touched and eaten with after he rose from the dead, was now rising upward, right in front of them, until a cloud swallowed him from view.

This was no ordinary cloud. Throughout the Old Testament, clouds represented the visible presence and glory of God. A cloud had covered Mount Sinai when God gave Moses the law. A cloud had filled the tabernacle and later Solomon's temple. And now that same kind of glorious cloud received Jesus as he entered heaven to take his throne at the right hand of God. This was the moment when the Father gave him all authority and crowned him as Lord and King. The kingdom the apostles had asked about was being inaugurated, not on an earthly throne in Jerusalem, but on a heavenly throne from which Jesus would rule over all things.

The apostles stood there, staring upward, trying to make sense of what they had just witnessed. And who could blame them? But while they were still gazing into the sky, two men in white clothing appeared beside them. These were angels, and they had a message.

"Men of Galilee," they said, "why do you stand here looking into the sky? This same Jesus, who has been taken from you into heaven, will come back in the same way you have seen him go into heaven" (1:11).

Two things matter here. First, the angels gently corrected the disciples. There was no point in staring at the sky. Jesus had given them work to do, and standing on a hilltop wasn't getting it done. Second, the angels gave them a promise. Jesus would return. The same Jesus, in the same visible, physical way, would come back one day. The departure was real, but it was not permanent.

THE UPPER ROOM

The apostles did exactly what Jesus told them to do. They returned to Jerusalem, about three-quarters of a mile walk from the Mount of Olives, and gathered in an upper room. Luke lists all eleven by name: Peter, John, James, Andrew, Philip, Thomas, Bartholomew, Matthew, James the son of Alphaeus, Simon the Zealot, and Judas the son of James. Also with them were certain women who had followed Jesus, Mary his mother, and his brothers.

And what did they do? They prayed. Together. Constantly. With one mind and one purpose.

This is the picture Luke wants you to see before the story takes off. A small group of about 120 believers, gathered in a room in Jerusalem, praying and waiting for a promise they didn't fully understand. They had no money. They had no political influence. They had no army. They had been given a mission to reach the ends of the earth, and they were starting with nothing but each other, a promise, and a prayer.

But they were about to receive the one thing that would make all the difference.

THE TWELFTH MAN

Before the Spirit came, there was one piece of unfinished business. Judas Iscariot, the disciple who had betrayed Jesus, was dead. He had purchased a field with the money he received for his treachery, and there he met a gruesome end. His position among the twelve apostles was empty.

Peter stood up and addressed the group. He pointed to passages in the Psalms that spoke of a man whose dwelling place would be left desolate and whose position another should take. Peter saw in these words a prophecy fulfilled by Judas and a clear instruction for what should happen next. Then he laid out the requirements for a replacement. The new apostle had to be someone who had been with them the entire time, from the days of John's baptism all the way through to the ascension. Most importantly, this person had to be a witness to the resurrection of Jesus (1:21–22).

That was the heart of the matter. The twelve apostles existed, above all else, to testify that Jesus was alive.

The group put forward two men who met these qualifications: Joseph, called Barsabbas, and Matthias. Then they prayed. "Lord, you know everyone's heart," they said. "Show us which of these two you have chosen" (1:24). They cast lots, and the lot fell to Matthias, who was then numbered with the eleven, bringing the total back to twelve.

Why did the number matter? Because Jesus had originally chosen twelve apostles to represent the twelve tribes of Israel. The full number was a signal that God was doing something with his people, and it required every appointed witness in place before it could begin. The eleven needed to become twelve again. And they needed the Lord himself to make the choice, not a committee vote.

The stage is now set. The twelve apostles are assembled. The prayers are rising. Jerusalem is waiting.

WHAT THIS MEANS FOR US

First, the mission continues through ordinary people. Jesus didn't assign the task of reaching the world to angels or to some heavenly army. He handed it to a small group of frightened, imperfect human beings. That's still how he works. God uses people like you and me to carry his message forward. You don't have to be powerful or famous or have everything figured out. You just have to be willing.

Second, waiting is not wasting time. The apostles were eager to get moving, but Jesus told them to wait. Sometimes the most faithful thing you can do is slow down and prepare your heart. Rushing ahead of God's timing doesn't show faith; it shows impatience. The disciples used their waiting time to pray, and that prayer shaped them into the people they needed to be for what was coming.

Third, God's plans are always bigger than ours. The apostles wanted a kingdom for Israel. Jesus gave them a mission for the world. It's easy to ask God for small, comfortable things when he has something far greater in mind. When his answer doesn't match your question, pay attention. He might be redirecting you toward something better than you ever imagined.

Fourth, Jesus is coming back. The angels made this promise, and nothing in the centuries since has changed it. Jesus ascended visibly and physically, and he will return in the same way. That promise shapes how we live right now. We are not waiting aimlessly. We are working and watching for a king who keeps his word.

TALKING POINTS

1. **The disciples asked Jesus about restoring Israel's kingdom, and he redirected their attention to a worldwide mission.** Why do you think it's hard for people to see beyond their own group or their own country to care about what God might be doing across the world?

2. **Jesus told the apostles to wait in Jerusalem before starting their mission.** When has waiting been difficult for

you? What did you learn during a time when you had to be patient before moving forward?

3. **The apostles, along with the women and Jesus' family, spent their waiting time in prayer together.** What do you think happens in a group of people when they pray with one mind and one purpose? How is that different from praying alone?

4. **Peter said the replacement for Judas had to be someone who had been with them from the beginning and could testify to Jesus' resurrection.** Why was eyewitness testimony so important for the early church? What kind of "witnessing" do Christians do today?

5. **Acts 1:8 lays out a roadmap for the spread of the gospel: Jerusalem, Judea and Samaria, and the ends of the earth.** If you were to create a similar roadmap for sharing your faith, what would the stages look like? Where would you start, and how far would you go?

The twelve are in place. The prayers are rising. The promise is almost here. But nothing can happen until the power comes down.

Turn the page.

2

THE DAY EVERYTHING CHANGED

Night at the Museum starts with a simple premise: every night, when the doors close and the lights go out, everything in the Museum of Natural History comes to life. The massive T. rex skeleton shakes itself free and chases a ball down the hallway. The tiny Roman soldiers wage war from their diorama. Attila the Hun storms through the corridors. What had been frozen and silent all day long is suddenly, impossibly alive.

Larry Daley, the new night guard, has no idea what he has walked into. He tries to keep order, but you can't control what happens when the power shows up. Every exhibit that had been standing still for years is now moving, speaking, and acting. The building looks the same from the outside, but inside, everything has changed.

That is a surprisingly good picture of what happened in Acts 2. A small group of men had been sitting in an upper room in Jerusalem, waiting, praying, doing nothing that would attract the attention of the thousands of pilgrims in the streets below. From the outside, nothing looked remarkable. But when the power of God arrived, that room exploded with life. Men who had been ordinary and silent were suddenly speaking in languages they had never learned, proclaiming the wonders of God to bewildered crowds. The building looked the same. The people inside were transformed. And just like Larry Daley, the watching world had no idea what to make of it.

WHEN THE DAY ARRIVED

The Jewish calendar had three great festivals each year that required every male to travel to Jerusalem: Passover, the Feast of Weeks, and the Feast of Tabernacles. The Feast of Weeks came fifty days after Passover, and for this reason it was also called by its name in the language of the day: Pentecost, meaning "fiftieth." It was originally a celebration of the firstfruits of the wheat harvest, a day of thanksgiving for God's provision. By the first century, it was also connected to the anniversary of God giving the law to Moses on Mount Sinai.

This meant that Jerusalem was packed. Devout Jews from every corner of the known world had made the pilgrimage to the holy city. Thousands upon thousands of people filled the streets, the temple courts, and every available lodging place. It was into this crowded, buzzing city that the Spirit was about to arrive.

Luke tells us that "when the day of Pentecost had fully come, they were all together in one place" (2:1). The apostles, all twelve of them, were gathered together just as Jesus had instructed. They had been waiting. Praying. And now the waiting was over.

What happened next was sudden and overwhelming.

First came a sound from heaven like a violent, rushing wind. It filled the entire house where the apostles were sitting. Then something appeared that looked like tongues of fire, and these separated and came to rest on each of the twelve. And they were all filled with the Holy Spirit and began to speak in languages they had never learned, as the Spirit gave them the ability (2:2–4).

This was the moment Jesus had promised. "You will be baptized with the Holy Spirit," he had told them. John the Baptist had baptized people by immersing them in water, but now the Spirit of God immersed the apostles in divine power. Their minds were supernaturally equipped with knowledge they had never studied, and their mouths spoke words they had never practiced. It was miraculous and unmistakable, and it happened right there in the heart of Jerusalem, on a day when the whole nation had gathered.

The timing was no accident. God chose the day of the firstfruits for the first harvest of the gospel.

AMAZEMENT AND MOCKERY

The sound drew a crowd. Jews from all over the world, men who had been born in places like Mesopotamia, Cappadocia, Egypt, Libya, Rome, Crete, and Arabia, rushed to see what was happening. And what they found stunned them. These Galilean men, who should have known nothing beyond their own regional dialect, were speaking clearly and fluently in languages from across the empire.

"How is this possible?" they asked each other. "Aren't all these men Galileans? Then how is it that each of us hears them in our own native language?" (2:7–8). They were hearing the wonders of God declared in their own tongues by men who had no natural ability to speak them.

The crowd was bewildered. Some were genuinely amazed and wanted to understand what this meant. Others, though, took the easy way out. "They've had too much wine," they sneered (2:13).

But mockery doesn't change facts. Something extraordinary had happened, and it demanded an explanation.

PETER STANDS UP

That explanation came from Peter.

Think about where Peter was just seven weeks earlier. On the night Jesus was arrested, Peter had followed him to the courtyard of the high priest. Three times he was asked if he was one of Jesus' followers. Three times he denied it. The last time, he swore with an oath that he didn't even know the man. When the rooster crowed, Peter went outside and wept bitterly.

Now look at him.

"Peter stood up with the eleven, raised his voice, and addressed the crowd" (2:14). This is not the same terrified man who couldn't face a servant girl's question. This is a man filled with the Holy Spirit, standing before thousands, and speaking with a boldness that would have been impossible without the power he had just received.

He started by swatting away the mockery. "These men aren't drunk," he said. "It's only nine in the morning." Then he got to the real point.

"This is what was spoken by the prophet Joel," Peter declared. And he quoted a prophecy that promised God would pour out his Spirit on all kinds of people, sons and daughters, young and old, and that everyone who calls on the name of the

Lord would be saved (2:16–21). What the crowd was witnessing, Peter explained, was the fulfillment of that ancient promise. The last days had begun.

But Peter wasn't just explaining a miracle. He was building a case, and the case was about Jesus.

THE SERMON THAT CHANGED THE WORLD

Peter laid out the facts like a man who had been trained by the greatest teacher who ever lived, because he had. He told the crowd three things about Jesus of Nazareth.

First, Jesus had been approved by God through miracles, wonders, and signs that they themselves had witnessed (2:22). This was not new information. Many in the crowd had seen what Jesus did during his ministry. They knew he was no ordinary man.

Second, this same Jesus had been handed over to them by God's deliberate plan, and they, with the help of wicked men, had nailed him to a cross and killed him (2:23). Peter did not soften this. He placed the guilt squarely on the shoulders of his audience. You did this. You killed the one God sent.

Third, God raised him from the dead (2:24). Death could not hold him. Peter then pointed to Psalm 16, where David had written, "You will not abandon my soul to the grave, nor will you let your Holy One see decay." David couldn't have been talking about himself, Peter argued, because David died and was buried, and his tomb was still there in Jerusalem for anyone to visit. David was speaking as a prophet about the Messiah, the one God had promised would sit on David's throne forever. That Messiah was Jesus, and God had raised him from the dead (2:25–32).

But Peter didn't stop with the resurrection. He went further. Jesus had not only risen; he had also ascended to the right hand of God and been crowned as Lord and King. It was from that throne of authority that he had now poured out the Holy Spirit, which was the very thing the crowd was seeing and hearing (2:33). Peter quoted one more passage, Psalm 110, where David wrote, "The Lord said to my Lord, sit at my right hand until I make your enemies your footstool." David didn't ascend to heaven, Peter pointed out. But Jesus did.

Then came the conclusion, and it hit like a thunderbolt.

"Therefore let all the house of Israel know for certain that God has made this Jesus, whom you crucified, both Lord and Christ" (2:36).

The man you killed is alive. He is seated on the throne of the universe. He is the Messiah. And his kingdom has begun.

WHAT SHALL WE DO?

Peter's words cut straight to the heart. Luke tells us the crowd was "pierced to the heart" and cried out to Peter and the other apostles, "Brothers, what shall we do?" (2:37).

This is the most important question anyone has ever asked. These people now believed that Jesus was the Christ. They knew they were guilty of his death. And they were desperate to know how to be saved.

Peter's answer was clear and direct. "Repent and be baptized, every one of you, in the name of Jesus Christ, for the forgiveness of your sins, and you will receive the gift of the Holy Spirit" (2:38).

Notice what Peter said, and notice what he didn't say. He did not tell them to believe, because they already believed.

Their very question proved it. No one asks, "What shall we do?" about a man they think is a fraud. Peter took them where they were—as believers pierced with guilt—and told them the two things they still needed to do: repent and be immersed (baptism). Repentance means a genuine change of mind and will, a decision to turn away from sin. Immersion in the name of Jesus was the act by which their sins would be forgiven, and they were promised the gift of the Holy Spirit in return.

Peter also told them that this promise was not just for them. It extended to their children, to future generations, and to "all who are far off," meaning everyone God would call through the gospel in the years and centuries to come (2:39).

About three thousand people responded that day. They believed the message, repented, and were immersed. On the day that the church was born, three thousand souls were added to the number of the saved.

A NEW KIND OF COMMUNITY

The chapter doesn't end with a number. It ends with a portrait. Luke describes what the new community of believers looked like in those earliest days, and the picture is extraordinary.

"They devoted themselves to the apostles' teaching, to fellowship, to the breaking of bread, and to prayers" (2:42).

These four things formed the heartbeat of the early church. The apostles taught, and the new disciples listened and learned. They shared life together, caring for each other's needs with a generosity that shocked the world around them. They broke bread together, sharing in the Lord's Supper as Jesus had commanded. And they prayed, constantly and fervently.

The result was a community unlike anything the ancient world had ever seen. Those who had property sold it and shared the proceeds with anyone who had a need. They spent time in the temple and in each other's homes, eating together with glad and sincere hearts, praising God, and enjoying the goodwill of the people around them (2:44–47).

And every day, the Lord added to their number those who were being saved.

This is what the Spirit produced. Not just miracles and tongues and fire, though those were real and important. The Spirit produced a community of people whose lives were transformed from the inside out, people who cared for one another, studied the Scriptures, worshiped God, and told everyone who would listen about the risen Jesus.

WHAT THIS MEANS FOR US

First, the gospel demands a response. Peter didn't just tell the crowd interesting facts about Jesus. He told them the truth about what they had done and what God had done, and then he told them what to do about it. The gospel is not information to be admired from a distance. It is a message that requires belief, repentance, and obedience. When Peter said "repent and be baptized for the forgiveness of your sins," he was showing the crowd the door and telling them to walk through it.

Second, God's power shows up where human ability runs out. Peter was a fisherman, not a trained public speaker. He had denied Jesus in front of a servant girl. Yet filled with the Spirit, he preached the sermon that launched the church.

God loves to work through people who know they aren't enough on their own, because that's when his power is most clearly on display.

Third, the church is not a building or a program. It's a community. The first believers didn't have a website, million-dollar marketing, or a strategy team. They had the apostles' teaching, fellowship, the Lord's Supper, and prayer. Those four things, received with devotion and lived out with generosity, were enough to turn the Roman Empire upside down. They are still enough today.

Fourth, the promise hasn't expired. Peter said the promise of forgiveness and the Holy Spirit was for his audience, for their children, and for all who are far off. That includes you and me. The same message, the same conditions, and the same promise still stand, two thousand years later.

TALKING POINTS

1. **Peter had denied Jesus three times just weeks before Pentecost.** What do you think changed in him between that night and the day he stood up to preach to thousands? What does his transformation tell us about second chances?

2. **Peter told the crowd to "repent and be baptized for the forgiveness of your sins."** Why do you think both repentance and baptism were part of his answer? What role does each one play in a person's response to the gospel?

3. **The early church devoted themselves to four things: teaching, fellowship, breaking bread, and prayer.** Which of these four do you think is most neglected by Christians today? Why do you think all four matter?

4. **The crowd at Pentecost had two very different reactions: some were amazed and wanted to know more, while others mocked and said the apostles were drunk.** Why do you think the same event can produce such opposite responses in people?

5. **Luke says the early believers shared everything they had with anyone who was in need.** What would it look like for a group of Christians today to live with that kind of generosity? What makes it hard?

Three thousand people woke up that morning as ordinary pilgrims in Jerusalem. By the end of the day, they were part of a brand-new community, forgiven, filled with the Spirit, and devoted to a risen King.

But not everyone in Jerusalem was happy about it. The same religious leaders who had handed Jesus over to be crucified were watching. And they were about to push back.

Turn the page.

3

UNSCHOOLED AND ORDINARY

Have you ever been the person nobody expected anything from? Maybe you were the youngest kid on the team, the one the coach put in only because the rules said everyone had to play. Or the new student who sat in the back of the class while everyone else already had their friend groups figured out. Or the kid who raised a hand to answer a question and watched the whole room turn around in surprise because nobody thought you would know.

There is a particular sting that comes with being underestimated. People look at you, size you up, and decide you don't have much to offer. They don't say it out loud, but you can feel it. You can see it in the way they pass you over, talk around you, or act surprised when you do something well.

But there is also a particular kind of satisfaction that comes when you prove everyone wrong. Not because you are showing off, but because you had something inside you that they couldn't see.

That is exactly what happened when Peter and John stood before the most powerful court in Israel. The members of the

Sanhedrin looked at these two men and saw nothing but "unschooled, ordinary men" (4:13). No rabbinical training. No credentials. No connections. Fishermen from Galilee, standing where only scholars and priests were supposed to stand.

But the court noticed something it couldn't explain. These ordinary men spoke with extraordinary boldness. And then the members of the Sanhedrin realized why: "they took note that these men had been with Jesus" (4:13).

That explained everything. Peter and John hadn't attended the finest schools. But they had spent three years walking with the Son of God, forty days learning from the risen Lord, and they were now filled with his Spirit. The people who underestimated them had missed the one thing that mattered most.

SOMETHING BETTER THAN MONEY

Not long after Pentecost, Peter and John were heading to the temple for the afternoon hour of prayer. At the gate called Beautiful, a man sat begging. He had been unable to walk since the day he was born, over forty years earlier. Every single day, someone carried him to this spot so he could ask for spare change from the worshipers passing by. That was his life. Sitting. Asking. Hoping for a handful of coins.

When he saw Peter and John, he held out his hand and asked them for money. Peter stopped, looked straight at him, and said something the man never expected to hear. "Silver and gold I do not have, but what I do have I give you. In the name of Jesus Christ of Nazareth, rise up and walk" (3:6).

Peter reached down, took the man by his right hand, and pulled him to his feet. Instantly, strength flooded into his feet and ankles. He didn't stumble. He didn't wobble. He stood. He walked. Then he leaped. And he went into the temple with them, jumping and shouting praises to God at the top of his lungs (3:7–8).

Everyone recognized him. This was the beggar who had sat at the Beautiful Gate for decades. And now he was standing on his own two feet, clinging to Peter and John and praising God. A massive crowd gathered in Solomon's Porch, and every face was stunned.

Peter seized the moment. "Why are you staring at us as if we made this man walk by our own power or godliness?" he asked (3:12). The power wasn't theirs. It was the power of the name of Jesus, the same Jesus they had handed over to Pilate and rejected, the Holy and Righteous One, the Author of life. God had raised him from the dead, and the apostles were witnesses.

Then Peter drove the point home with a piercing contrast: you killed the Author of life, but God raised him from the dead. And it is through faith in his name that this man you see standing here has been made completely well.

Peter called on the crowd to repent and turn to God so that their sins might be wiped away. The message echoed what he had preached at Pentecost, and it had the same explosive effect. About five thousand men believed (4:4). The church was growing at an astonishing rate.

FISHERMEN ON TRIAL

The Sadducees were furious. As the party that controlled the temple and denied the resurrection, they could not tolerate these men using their temple courts to proclaim that a dead man had come back to life. They had Peter and John arrested and thrown into jail for the night.

The next morning, the full Sanhedrin assembled. This was the highest religious court in the nation, the same body that had condemned Jesus to death just weeks earlier. Annas the high priest was there. Caiaphas was there. The most powerful men in Israel sat in a semicircle, and two fishermen from Galilee were brought out to stand before them.

"By what power or by what name did you do this?" they demanded (4:7).

Peter, filled with the Holy Spirit, gave them an answer they did not want to hear. "It is by the name of Jesus Christ of Nazareth, whom you crucified, whom God raised from the dead, that this man stands before you healed" (4:10). Then he added a line that must have made the room go silent: "Salvation is found in no one else, for there is no other name under heaven given to mankind by which we must be saved" (4:12).

Luke tells us two things about the Sanhedrin's reaction. First, they recognized that Peter and John were "unschooled, ordinary men," and they were astonished at their boldness. Second, they noticed that these men had been with Jesus (4:13). That explained everything. These fishermen had no rabbinical training. But they had spent three years walking with Jesus, forty days learning from the risen Lord, and they were now filled with his Spirit. That combination turned ordinary men into the most formidable witnesses the world had ever seen.

And there was one more problem for the court. The healed man was standing right there beside the apostles, on feet that had never worked before. You can argue with a sermon. You can dismiss a claim. But you cannot argue with a man who is standing on legs that were useless for forty years. "Seeing the man who had been healed standing beside them, they could say nothing against it" (4:14).

So they did the only thing they could think of. They threatened. "Do not speak or teach at all in the name of Jesus," they ordered (4:18).

Peter and John's reply is one of the boldest statements in all of Scripture: "Which is right in God's eyes: to listen to you, or to him? You be the judges! As for us, we cannot help speaking about what we have seen and heard" (4:19–20).

The Sanhedrin released them with more threats but could not punish them, because the people were praising God for the miracle.

A PRAYING CHURCH

When Peter and John returned to the other Christians and reported what had happened, the group did not panic. They did not form a political strategy or hire lawyers. They prayed.

And what a prayer it was. They didn't ask God to remove the opposition. They asked him for boldness to keep speaking in the face of it. "Now, Lord, consider their threats and enable your servants to speak your word with great boldness," they said. "Stretch out your hand to heal and perform signs and wonders through the name of your holy servant Jesus" (4:29–30).

When they finished praying, the place where they were meeting was shaken. They were all filled with the Holy Spirit, and they spoke the word of God boldly (4:31). God answered their prayer on the spot.

The community that emerged from this season was remarkable. Luke tells us that the believers were "one in heart and mind" (4:32). No one claimed that their possessions belonged only to them. Those who owned land or houses sold them and brought the money to the apostles to distribute to anyone in need. This was not forced. Nobody was required to sell anything. It was voluntary generosity, overflowing from hearts transformed by the Spirit.

A man named Joseph, whom the apostles nicknamed Barnabas (which means "son of encouragement"), sold a field he owned and laid the money at the apostles' feet. We will hear much more about Barnabas later. For now, Luke introduces him as an example of what genuine, wholehearted devotion looked like in the early church.

A DANGEROUS LIE

But where genuine devotion exists, counterfeits will try to slip in.

A married couple named Ananias and Sapphira sold a piece of property. They kept part of the money for themselves, which was perfectly within their rights. The problem was not what they kept. The problem was what they pretended. They brought a portion of the proceeds and laid it at the apostles' feet as though it were the full amount. They wanted the reputation of total sacrifice without the actual cost.

Peter confronted Ananias directly. "Why has Satan filled your heart to lie to the Holy Spirit and to keep back part of the price of the land?" he asked. "While it remained unsold, wasn't it yours? And after it was sold, wasn't the money at your disposal? You have not lied to men. You have lied to God" (5:3–4).

Notice what Peter said. The property belonged to Ananias. The money was his to do with as he pleased. No one had forced him to give anything. His sin was not in keeping some of the money. His sin was in pretending he had given it all. He treated the Holy Spirit as someone who could be fooled.

When Ananias heard these words, he fell down dead. About three hours later, Sapphira arrived, not knowing what had happened to her husband. Peter gave her a chance to tell the truth. She didn't take it. She repeated the same lie and met the same fate (5:7–10).

This is one of the most sobering passages in the entire Bible. Great fear came upon the whole church and everyone who heard about it (5:11). And it should make us pause too. God was not punishing imperfect generosity. He was judging deliberate deception at the very moment when the church's integrity and the apostles' authority were being established before the watching world. If their lie had gone unchallenged, it would have undermined the foundation of trust on which the entire young church was being built. The severity of the judgment reflected the seriousness of the threat.

UNSTOPPABLE

The apostles continued performing signs and wonders among the people. The sick were carried into the streets on mats, hoping that even Peter's shadow might fall on them as he passed by. People streamed in from surrounding towns, bringing the sick and those tormented by unclean spirits, and all of them were healed (5:15–16).

The high priest and the Sadducees had seen enough. Filled with jealousy, they arrested all the apostles this time and locked them in the public jail.

But during the night, an angel of the Lord opened the prison doors and led them out. "Go, stand in the temple courts," the angel said, "and tell the people all about this new life" (5:20). So at daybreak, the apostles walked right back into the temple and began teaching again.

When the Sanhedrin sent officers to bring the prisoners from the jail, they found the doors securely locked, the guards standing at their posts, and the cells completely empty. While the court was still trying to make sense of this bewildering news, someone rushed in to report, "The men you put in jail are standing in the temple courts teaching the people" (5:25).

The apostles were brought before the Sanhedrin a second time. "We gave you strict orders not to teach in this name," the high priest said. "Yet you have filled Jerusalem with your teaching" (5:28).

Peter's answer was simple and unshakeable: "We must obey God rather than human beings" (5:29). Then he preached Jesus to them one more time: God raised him from the dead after they had killed him by hanging him on a cross. God exalted him to his own right hand as Prince and Savior, to give repentance and forgiveness of sins to Israel. "We are witnesses of these things," Peter said, "and so is the Holy Spirit, whom God has given to those who obey him" (5:32).

The court was enraged. Some wanted to kill the apostles on the spot. But a Pharisee named Gamaliel, one of the most respected teachers in the nation, stood up and urged caution. He reminded the council of other movements that had risen and collapsed on their own when their leaders died. "Leave these men alone," he said. "If their purpose or activity is of human origin, it will fail. But if it is from God, you will not be able to stop these men; you will only find yourselves fighting against God" (5:38–39).

The Sanhedrin took his advice, at least partially. They had the apostles flogged and ordered them once more never to speak in the name of Jesus. Then they released them.

And the apostles? They left the Sanhedrin "rejoicing because they had been counted worthy of suffering disgrace for the Name" (5:41). This was the first time the followers of Jesus suffered physical punishment for their faith. They wore the bruises like a badge of honor.

Day after day, in the temple courts and from house to house, they never stopped teaching and proclaiming the good news that Jesus is the Christ (5:42).

Threats did not stop them. Prison did not stop them. A beating did not stop them. The more the authorities pushed back, the more the gospel advanced.

WHAT THIS MEANS FOR US

First, what matters most cannot be bought. Peter had no money to give the lame man. But what he did have—the name and authority of Jesus—was worth infinitely more than silver or gold. The most valuable thing you can offer another person is not material. It is the truth about Jesus. That is something poverty can never take from you and wealth can never replace.

Second, obedience to God comes before obedience to people. Peter and John did not disrespect the Sanhedrin out of rebellion. They recognized that when human authority directly contradicts God's authority, God wins. This does not mean we ignore every rule we dislike. It means that when someone tells us to disobey God, we must politely, firmly, and courageously say no.

Third, integrity matters more than image. Ananias and Sapphira wanted to look generous without actually being generous. They cared more about what people thought of them than about what God knew about them. Pretending to be something you are not is always a dangerous path, especially when the one you are trying to fool is God himself.

Fourth, opposition does not mean failure. The apostles were arrested, threatened, jailed, and beaten. By the world's standards, things were going badly. But by God's standards, the mission was exactly on track. The church grew after every wave of opposition. If you are doing the right thing and facing resistance, that does not necessarily mean you have made a mistake. Sometimes it means you are exactly where you are supposed to be.

TALKING POINTS

1. **Peter told the lame man, "Silver and gold I do not have, but what I do have I give you."** What did Peter have that was more valuable than money? What do you have that you could offer someone in need, even if it is not money?

2. **The Sanhedrin was amazed that Peter and John were "unschooled, ordinary men."** Why do you think God so often chooses to work through people the world considers unqualified? What does this tell us about where real power comes from?

3. **Ananias and Sapphira were not punished for keeping some of their money but for lying about it.** Why do you think dishonesty inside the church was treated so seriously? What does this teach us about honesty in our relationship with God?

4. **Gamaliel told the Sanhedrin, "If it is from God, you will not be able to stop it."** Do you think his advice was wise? How does the fact that the church is still here two thousand years later connect to what he said?

5. **After being beaten, the apostles left "rejoicing because they had been counted worthy of suffering disgrace for the Name."** How is it possible to feel joy while suffering? What would it take for someone to have that kind of attitude?

The church was growing. The apostles were bold. Even the threats and the fists of the most powerful court in the land could not slow the gospel down. But growth always brings new challenges. The church was about to face a problem it had not dealt with before: not an attack from the outside, but a complaint rising up from within.

Turn the page.

4

THE MAN WITH THE FACE OF AN ANGEL

Akeelah Anderson is an eleven-year-old girl from South Los Angeles, and she has a secret. She's brilliant. But in her neighborhood, being smart isn't exactly cool, so she hides it. She skips class. She keeps her head down. Nobody expects much from her.

Then a reclusive college professor named Dr. Larabee sees what everyone else has missed. He recognizes her gift and begins coaching her for the Scripps National Spelling Bee. The road is brutal. Akeelah faces doubt from her classmates, resistance from her mother, and the constant pressure of being a girl from a tough neighborhood competing against kids with every advantage money can buy. But she keeps going.

And in the film's climactic moment, Akeelah stands on a national stage, alone under the lights, one girl against the best spellers in the country. She spells the word. She and her rival end up sharing the championship. The crowd erupts.

Akeelah and the Bee is a story about a person who was chosen for something ordinary and turned out to be extraordinary. That's exactly what happens to a man named Stephen in Acts

6–7. He was chosen to help distribute food to widows. Nobody picked him to be the church's first great defender of the faith. But when Stephen stepped onto the biggest stage of his life, standing before the highest court in Israel, he delivered the longest and most sweeping speech in the entire book of Acts.

The difference is that Stephen's story doesn't end with applause.

It ends with stones.

A PROBLEM INSIDE

Up to this point, the church had faced threats from the outside: arrests, trials, beatings, and orders to be silent. But in Acts 6, the trouble came from within.

The church in Jerusalem had been growing rapidly, and with growth came growing pains. Two groups existed in the community: the Hebraic Jews, who spoke the local language and followed traditional customs, and the Hellenistic Jews, who came from other parts of the Roman world and spoke the common language of the empire. Both groups were Christians. Both belonged to the church. But the Hellenistic widows were being overlooked in the daily distribution of food (6:1). Whether this was intentional neglect or an honest oversight, the result was a real complaint from a real group of people who were being left behind.

The twelve apostles responded wisely. They didn't dismiss the concern, and they didn't try to handle everything themselves. "It would not be right for us to neglect the ministry of the word of God in order to wait on tables," they said (6:2). Instead, they told the whole church to select seven men of good reputation, full of the Spirit and wisdom, who could be put in charge of this daily distribution. The apostles would continue to devote themselves to prayer and the ministry of the word.

The entire community agreed. They chose seven men, all of whom had names suggesting Hellenistic backgrounds. This was a remarkable decision. The people being served were Hellenistic, so the church chose Hellenistic leaders to oversee the work. It was a display of trust, humility, and genuine concern for those who had been neglected.

The first name on the list was Stephen, a man described as "full of faith and the Holy Spirit" (6:5). He was chosen to serve tables. But God had something far bigger in mind for him.

MORE THAN A TABLE SERVER

Stephen's gifts went well beyond food distribution. Luke tells us he was "full of God's grace and power" and that he performed great wonders and signs among the people (6:8). He was also a fearless speaker. When members of a Hellenistic synagogue in Jerusalem began to argue with him, they could not stand up against the wisdom and the Spirit by which he spoke (6:10). Every argument they threw at him, he answered from the Scriptures with an authority that left them speechless.

Since they couldn't defeat him in debate, they decided to destroy him another way. They secretly persuaded men to lie about him, claiming they had heard him speak blasphemous words against Moses and against God (6:11). They stirred up the people and the elders and the teachers of the law, and they dragged Stephen before the Sanhedrin. False witnesses testified, "This man never stops speaking against this holy place and against the law" (6:13).

But as the members of the Sanhedrin stared at the accused man standing before them, they saw something unexpected. Stephen's face looked like the face of an angel (6:15).

A HISTORY LESSON NO ONE WANTED TO HEAR

The high priest asked Stephen a simple question: "Are these charges true?" (7:1).

What followed was not a typical defense. Stephen didn't argue about what he had or hadn't said. He didn't beg for mercy. Instead, he walked the entire Sanhedrin through the history of Israel, starting with Abraham and ending with a devastating accusation that left the court in a fury.

He began with Abraham, who was called by God to leave his homeland and go to a land he had never seen. Abraham obeyed without knowing where he was going. He never owned the land God promised him, but he trusted the promise anyway (7:2–8).

Then Stephen moved to Joseph. God was with Joseph, giving him wisdom and favor. But Joseph's own brothers, eaten by jealousy, sold him into slavery in Egypt. The very person God had chosen to save his family was the one his family rejected (7:9–16).

Then came Moses, and here Stephen spent the most time. Moses was raised in Pharaoh's palace and educated in all the wisdom of Egypt. When he tried to help his own people, they pushed him away. "Who made you ruler and judge over us?" they demanded (7:27). Moses fled to the wilderness. Forty years later, God appeared to him in a burning bush and sent him back to deliver Israel. And Moses did deliver them, performing wonders and signs in Egypt, at the Red Sea, and in the wilderness.

But did Israel follow him gratefully? No. They grumbled. They resisted. They told Aaron to make them a golden calf so they could worship an idol while Moses was on the mountain receiving God's law. The same people God was rescuing kept pushing away the very man God had sent to rescue them (7:35–43).

Stephen then turned to the tabernacle and the temple. God had given Moses instructions for a tabernacle, a portable tent where God's presence would dwell among his people. Later, Solomon built a permanent temple. But Stephen quoted the prophet Isaiah: "Heaven is my throne, and the earth is my footstool. What kind of house will you build for me? says the Lord. Or where will my resting place be? Has not my hand made all these things?" (7:49–50). God cannot be contained in a building made by human hands. He is bigger than any temple.

Do you see what Stephen was doing? He wasn't running from the charges against him. He was building a case against his accusers.

THE ACCUSATION

Everything Stephen had said was building to this moment. With the entire Sanhedrin staring at him, he looked at the most powerful religious leaders in Israel and said:

"You stiff-necked people! Your hearts and ears are still uncircumcised. You are just like your ancestors: you always resist the Holy Spirit! Was there ever a prophet your ancestors did not persecute? They even killed those who predicted the coming of the Righteous One. And now you have betrayed and murdered him. You who have received the law that was given through angels but have not obeyed it" (7:51–53).

Stephen's point was devastating. Israel's leaders were not the faithful guardians of God's truth they claimed to be. They were the latest link in a long chain of rebellion. Their ancestors rejected Joseph. Their ancestors rejected Moses. Their ancestors rejected the prophets. And now they had rejected and murdered the Righteous One himself, Jesus the Messiah. The same pattern that had repeated throughout all of Israel's history had reached its terrible climax in their generation.

Stephen was not blaspheming Moses or the law. He was showing that the Sanhedrin had violated Moses and the law by rejecting the very Messiah that Moses and the prophets had pointed to.

HEAVEN OPENS

The Sanhedrin erupted. Luke says they were "furious and gnashed their teeth at him" (7:54). But Stephen, filled with the Holy Spirit, looked up and saw something no one else in that room could see. "Look," he said, "I see heaven open and the Son of Man standing at the right hand of God" (7:56).

Standing. In nearly every other reference to Jesus at God's right hand, he is seated on his throne. But here, Stephen saw him *standing.* It was as though Jesus had risen from his throne to receive his faithful witness, to honor the man who refused to be silent even when silence would have saved his life.

The court exploded. Covering their ears and screaming, they rushed at Stephen, dragged him out of the city, and began to stone him (7:57–58). The witnesses laid their coats at the feet of a young man named Saul. Remember that name. You will hear it again.

As the stones crashed into his body, Stephen prayed two prayers. The first echoed Jesus on the cross: "Lord Jesus, receive my spirit" (7:59). The second was even more remarkable. Falling to his knees, with his final breath, Stephen cried out, "Lord, do not hold this sin against them" (7:60).

Then he died.

He was the first follower of Jesus to be killed for his faith. The church's first martyr. And he died exactly the way his Lord had died: with a prayer of forgiveness on his lips for the very people who were killing him.

WHAT THIS MEANS FOR US

First, God uses people where they are and takes them where they need to go. Stephen was chosen to serve food. God turned him into the church's first great apologist and its first martyr. You never know where faithful service in a small role will lead. The person who volunteers to help with the smallest task may be the one God is preparing for the biggest assignment.

Second, knowing the Bible is one of the most powerful things you can do. Stephen's speech is a masterclass in Scripture. He knew the story of Abraham, Joseph, Moses, David, and Solomon inside and out, and he could show how it all pointed to Jesus. When opposition came, Stephen didn't rely on his own cleverness. He relied on God's word. There is no substitute for knowing the Scriptures deeply and being ready to use them.

Third, telling the truth may cost you something. Stephen could have softened his message. He could have avoided the accusations in verses 51–53. He could have tried to save himself. But he chose faithfulness over safety. Not every truth is comfortable, and not every audience will appreciate hearing it. But the truth is still worth telling, even when the consequences are painful.

Fourth, forgiveness is the ultimate act of strength. Stephen's final prayer was not a curse on his killers. It was a plea for their forgiveness. That kind of response doesn't come from human willpower. It comes from a heart so full of the Spirit that even in the worst moment, it overflows with the character of Jesus. Forgiveness in the face of injustice is not weakness. It is the highest form of courage.

TALKING POINTS

1. **Stephen was chosen to help distribute food, but he ended up preaching the longest sermon in Acts.** What does his story teach us about being faithful in small responsibilities? Have you ever started with something small that turned into something bigger than you expected?

2. **Stephen's speech traced a pattern throughout Israel's history: God's people kept rejecting the messengers God sent to them.** Why do you think people so often resist the very ones who are trying to help them? Can you think of times when this still happens today?

3. **When the Sanhedrin looked at Stephen, they saw that his face was "like the face of an angel."** What do you think Luke wants us to understand about Stephen from that description? What does it say about the kind of person he was?

4. **Stephen saw heaven open and Jesus standing at the right hand of God.** Why do you think Jesus was standing

rather than sitting? What might that detail tell us about how Jesus responds when his followers suffer for him?

5. **Stephen's last words were a prayer asking God not to hold his killers' sin against them.** What kind of person can pray like that while being stoned to death? What would it take for you to forgive someone who had deeply hurt you?

Stephen was dead. His body lay outside the city walls. A young man named Saul stood nearby, approving of the execution, watching over the coats of the men who had thrown the stones.

But Stephen's death was not the end of the story. It was, in fact, the beginning of something the Sanhedrin never intended. A great wave of persecution was about to hit the church in Jerusalem, and that wave would scatter believers across the countryside like seeds thrown by a farmer's hand. Everywhere they landed, they would take root.

The gospel was about to break free from Jerusalem.

Turn the page.

5

SCATTERED SEEDS

Have you ever had a plan completely fall apart, only to discover later that the disaster turned into the best thing that could have happened?

Maybe your family had to move to a new city and you were furious about leaving your friends behind. But you got to the new school and made the best friend you've ever had. Or maybe you got cut from the team you wanted, signed up for something else out of frustration, and found out you were actually great at it. Life has a strange way of taking what looks like a catastrophe and turning it into a starting point for something you never would have chosen on your own.

That is exactly what happened to the early church in Acts 8–9. A wave of violent persecution crashed down on the believers in Jerusalem. Christians were dragged from their homes and thrown into prison. The community that had been "one in heart and mind" was torn apart, its members scattered like seeds flung from a farmer's hand. It looked like the end of everything.

It was actually the beginning of everything.

Because everywhere those scattered believers landed, they opened their mouths and preached Jesus. The persecution that was meant to crush the church became the very thing that spread it. The gospel was about to break out of Jerusalem and race across the map, carried by refugees who refused to stop talking about the risen King.

PHILIP GOES TO SAMARIA

The first person Luke follows out of Jerusalem is Philip, one of the seven men chosen to help distribute food to widows. Like Stephen before him, Philip turned out to be far more than a table server. Filled with the Spirit, he traveled north to a city in Samaria and began proclaiming the Messiah (8:5).

This was a radical step. Jews and Samaritans had despised each other for centuries. Samaritans were considered half-breeds and heretics. They worshiped on a different mountain and rejected much of the Jewish Scriptures. Most Jews would have walked miles out of their way just to avoid passing through Samaritan territory.

But Philip went straight to them with the gospel. And the Samaritans listened. The crowds paid close attention to what Philip said, especially when they saw the signs he performed. Evil spirits came out of people with shrieks, and those who were paralyzed or lame were healed. Luke says there was "great joy in that city" (8:8). The same Spirit who had set Jerusalem on fire at Pentecost was now doing the same work in Samaria.

A man named Simon had held power over the city for years through sorcery. The people called him "the Great Power of God" (8:10). But when Philip arrived preaching the kingdom of God and the name of Jesus Christ, the people turned from Simon and believed. Men and women were baptized. Even Simon himself believed and was baptized and began following Philip around, amazed by the signs he saw (8:13).

When the apostles in Jerusalem heard that Samaria had received the word of God, they sent Peter and John. The two apostles prayed for the Samaritan believers and laid hands on them, and they received the Holy Spirit (8:17). This was a momentous event. For the first time, the Spirit fell on people who were not Jews in Jerusalem. The wall between Jews and Samaritans was cracking under the weight of the gospel.

Simon, however, revealed the true state of his heart. When he saw that the Spirit was given through the laying on of the apostles' hands, he offered them money. "Give me this power too," he said, "so that anyone I lay hands on may receive the Holy Spirit" (8:19). Simon wanted the power of God as a tool for his own advancement.

Peter's rebuke was fierce. "May your money perish with you, because you thought you could buy the gift of God with money! You have no part or share in this ministry, for your heart is not right before God. Repent of this wickedness" (8:20–22). The gift of the Holy Spirit is not for sale. It cannot be purchased, earned, or manipulated. Simon wanted to control God's power. But God's power is not a product on a shelf. It is a gift from a throne.

A CHARIOT IN THE DESERT

The Spirit was not finished with Philip. An angel told him to leave the successful mission in Samaria and travel south, toward a desert road that ran from Jerusalem to Gaza. This must have seemed strange. Why leave a thriving work to walk into an empty wilderness?

Philip obeyed. And on that road he encountered a man who would have been an outsider in almost every way imaginable.

The man was an Ethiopian, a high-ranking official in charge of the entire treasury of Candace, the queen of Ethiopia. He was also a eunuch, which meant that under the law of Moses he would have been excluded from full participation in the worship of Israel (Deuteronomy 23:1). He had traveled all the way to Jerusalem to worship God, but the very temple he came to honor would have kept him at a distance. Now he was heading home, sitting in his chariot, reading aloud from the scroll of the prophet Isaiah.

The Spirit told Philip to go to that chariot and stay near it. Philip ran up alongside and heard the man reading from Isaiah 53: "He was led like a sheep to the slaughter, and as a lamb before its shearer is silent, so he does not open his mouth. In his humiliation he was deprived of justice. Who can speak of his descendants? For his life was taken from the earth."

"Do you understand what you're reading?" Philip asked.

"How can I," the man replied, "unless someone explains it to me?" (8:31). He invited Philip to climb up and sit beside him.

Then he asked the question that opened the door to everything: "Who is the prophet talking about? Himself, or someone else?" (8:34).

Beginning with that very passage, Philip told him the good news about Jesus. The Suffering Servant of Isaiah, the one who was led like a lamb to slaughter, the one whose life was taken from the earth, was Jesus of Nazareth. He had been rejected, crucified, and buried. But God raised him from the dead and exalted him to the highest throne. And through his sacrifice, forgiveness and new life were available to everyone who believed, even to those the old system had shut out.

As they traveled along the road, they came to some water. The eunuch said, "Look, here is water. What can stand in the way of my being baptized?" (8:36). Nothing. Nothing could stand in the way. Not his nationality. Not his physical condition. Not the old restrictions that had kept him at the margins.

They went down into the water, and Philip immersed him. When they came up out of the water, the Spirit of the Lord suddenly took Philip away, and the eunuch never saw him again. But he went on his way rejoicing (8:39).

The prophet Isaiah had once written that God would give eunuchs "a memorial and a name better than sons and daughters" (Isaiah 56:5). On a desert road, through the preaching of a scattered refugee, that ancient promise came true.

THE ENEMY

Meanwhile, a young man named Saul was tearing the church apart. Luke does not let us forget him. Saul had watched Stephen die and approved of his execution. Now he was "breathing out murderous threats against the Lord's disciples" (9:1). He went to the high priest and obtained letters authorizing him to travel to Damascus, about 135 miles northeast of Jerusalem, and arrest any followers of "the Way" he found there, men or women, and drag them back in chains.

Saul was not just a casual opponent. He was a zealot, utterly convinced that the followers of Jesus were a dangerous movement that needed to be destroyed. He had the credentials, the authority, and the fury to do it. If any single person seemed beyond the reach of the gospel, it was Saul of Tarsus.

But the risen Jesus had other plans.

LIGHT ON THE ROAD

As Saul neared Damascus, a light from heaven suddenly blazed around him, brighter than the midday sun. He fell to the ground. And he heard a voice.

"Saul, Saul, why are you persecuting me?" (9:4).

"Who are you, Lord?" Saul asked.

"I am Jesus, whom you are persecuting," the voice replied. "Now get up and go into the city, and you will be told what you must do" (9:5–6).

Those words changed everything. The man Saul was hunting for victims of the Way was now face down in the dirt, blinded by the glory of the very Lord he had been fighting against. The men traveling with him stood speechless. They heard the sound but saw no one. When Saul opened his eyes, he could see nothing. They had to take him by the hand and lead him into Damascus like a child.

For three days he sat in darkness. He did not eat. He did not drink. The man who had set out as the church's fiercest enemy had been stopped dead in his tracks by the church's risen Lord.

Notice what Jesus said: "Why are you persecuting *me*?" Not "why are you persecuting my followers," though that was what

Saul was doing. Jesus identified himself so closely with his people that an attack on them was an attack on him. To drag a Christian out of her home was to lay hands on Christ himself.

ANANIAS AND THE IMPOSSIBLE ERRAND

In Damascus, a disciple named Ananias received his own vision. The Lord told him to go to a house on Straight Street and ask for a man from Tarsus named Saul, who was praying and had seen a vision of Ananias coming to restore his sight.

Ananias was understandably terrified. "Lord," he said, "I have heard many reports about this man and all the harm he has done to your people in Jerusalem. And he has come here with authority to arrest all who call on your name" (9:13–14).

The Lord's answer was extraordinary. "Go! This man is my chosen instrument to carry my name before the Gentiles and their kings and before the people of Israel. I will show him how much he must suffer for my name" (9:15–16).

The man who had caused the most suffering was about to become the man who would suffer the most. Saul, the great persecutor, was being called to become the great missionary.

Ananias obeyed. He found Saul, placed his hands on him, and said, "Brother Saul, the Lord Jesus, who appeared to you on the road as you were coming here, has sent me so that you may see again and be filled with the Holy Spirit" (9:17). Something like scales fell from Saul's eyes. He could see. He got up and was baptized. Then he ate, and his strength returned (9:18–19).

The transformation was immediate and total. Saul began preaching in the synagogues of Damascus that Jesus is the Son of God (9:20). The people who heard him were astonished.

"Isn't this the man who raised havoc in Jerusalem?" they asked (9:21). But Saul grew more and more powerful in his message, proving from the Scriptures that Jesus was the Christ.

His former allies were furious. They plotted to kill him. Saul's friends helped him escape by lowering him in a basket through an opening in the city wall at night (9:25). When he arrived in Jerusalem, the Christians there were afraid of him too, until a man named Barnabas vouched for him and brought him to the apostles.

The church had peace. Judea, Galilee, and Samaria all had growing communities of believers. The word of God was spreading. And the man who had once tried to destroy it all was now one of its most passionate voices.

WHAT THIS MEANS FOR US

First, God turns disasters into deliveries. The persecution that scattered the church was meant to destroy it. Instead, it planted the gospel in new soil across the region. When your plans fall apart, God may be planting you somewhere you never expected to grow. The worst day of your life may turn out to be the first day of your most important work.

Second, the gospel breaks every barrier. Philip preached to Samaritans and baptized an Ethiopian eunuch. The walls of ethnicity, geography, and religious exclusion all came down before the name of Jesus. No one is too far away, too different, or too disqualified to be welcomed into the family of God.

Third, no one is beyond the reach of Jesus. If Saul of Tarsus, the church's worst enemy, could be stopped on a road and turned into the church's greatest missionary, then no heart is too hard for God to change. Never give up on someone just because they seem too far gone. The same Jesus who knocked Saul to the ground is still in the business of transforming lives.

Fourth, obedience often means doing what scares you. Ananias was told to go to the most dangerous man in the city and call him "brother." Philip was told to leave a successful ministry and walk into a desert. Both obeyed, and both became instruments of some of the most important conversions in history. The scariest assignment might be the most significant one.

TALKING POINTS

1. **The persecution that scattered the church actually helped the gospel spread faster.** Can you think of other examples, from history or your own life, where something painful ended up leading to something good?

2. **Philip baptized the Ethiopian eunuch even though Old Testament law had excluded eunuchs from full participation in worship.** What does this tell us about how the gospel changes who is welcome in the people of God?

3. **Jesus asked Saul, "Why are you persecuting me?"** What does it mean that Jesus identified an attack on his followers as an attack on himself? How should that shape the way we treat other believers?

4. **Ananias was told to go help the very man who had been arresting and imprisoning Christians.** What would it have taken for you to obey that kind of instruction? What does his obedience teach us about trusting God?

5. **Barnabas believed in Saul when everyone else was afraid of him.** Have you ever been the one person willing to

vouch for someone others didn't trust? Why is it important to have people like Barnabas in the church?

Seeds were flying. Samaria had received the word. An Ethiopian official was heading home with the gospel in his heart. And the church's greatest enemy had become its newest preacher.

But the biggest barrier of all was still standing. The gospel had reached Samaritans and a single eunuch on a desert road. It had not yet broken through to the Gentile world. That wall was about to come down, and the man who would swing the hammer was the last person anyone would have expected.

Turn the page.

6

THE WALL COMES DOWN

Jane Austen's *Pride and Prejudice* opens with one of the most famous sentences in all of English literature: "It is a truth universally acknowledged, that a single man in possession of a good fortune, must be in want of a wife." But the real story isn't about marriage. It's about two people who are completely wrong about each other.

Elizabeth Bennet meets Mr. Darcy at a party and immediately dislikes him. He's proud, cold, and dismissive. Darcy, for his part, looks down on Elizabeth's family as beneath his social standing. Both of them are convinced they have the other person figured out. And both of them are wrong. It takes almost the entire novel for their walls of prejudice to come crumbling down, and when they finally do, what emerges is something neither of them expected: understanding, respect, and love where there had once been contempt.

Walls of prejudice are not just a problem in English novels. They have been a human problem since the beginning, and in Acts 10 11, the church ran headlong into one of the tallest walls in the ancient world: the barrier between Jews and

Gentiles. For centuries, faithful Jews had avoided entering the homes of non-Jews, eating their food, or sharing their tables. The law of Moses had drawn sharp lines between clean and unclean, and over time those lines had hardened into an impassable wall.

God was about to tear that wall down. And the man he chose to swing the first blow was the last person who would have volunteered for the job.

A ROMAN SOLDIER WHO PRAYED

The story begins in Caesarea, the Roman capital of Judea, with a man named Cornelius. He was a centurion in the Italian Regiment, a Roman military officer in charge of about one hundred soldiers. By every measure that mattered in the Jewish world, he was an outsider. He was a Gentile. He wore Roman armor. He served the empire that occupied Jewish land and collected Jewish taxes.

But Cornelius was no ordinary Roman. Luke describes him as devout, God-fearing, generous to the poor, and faithful in prayer (10:2). He believed in the God of Israel and lived accordingly, but he had never taken the full step of becoming a Jewish convert. He stood at the edge of the faith, close enough to see the beauty of it but never fully welcomed inside.

One afternoon around three o'clock, the hour of prayer, Cornelius had a vision. An angel appeared to him and called him by name. "Your prayers and gifts to the poor have come up as a memorial offering before God," the angel told him (10:4). Then the angel gave him specific instructions: send men to the city of Joppa, about thirty miles down the coast, and find a man named Simon Peter, who was staying at the house of Simon the tanner by the sea.

Cornelius obeyed immediately. He sent two servants and a devout soldier to fetch Peter. He had no idea what message Peter would bring. He only knew that God himself had told him to send for this man.

A SHEET FROM HEAVEN

The next day, while the messengers were still traveling toward Joppa, Peter went up on the flat rooftop of Simon the tanner's house to pray. It was about noon. He was hungry, and while a meal was being prepared below, he fell into a trance.

He saw heaven open. A large sheet, held by its four corners, descended toward him. Inside the sheet was a collection of animals: four-footed creatures, reptiles, and birds. Some of them were animals that the law of Moses had declared unclean. No faithful Jew would touch them, much less eat them.

Then a voice spoke: "Get up, Peter. Kill and eat" (10:13).

Peter was horrified. "Surely not, Lord!" he said. "I have never eaten anything impure or unclean" (10:14). Peter had kept the dietary laws his entire life. He was not about to abandon them now, not even at the command of a voice from heaven.

But the voice answered: "Do not call anything impure that God has made clean" (10:15).

This happened three times. Three times the sheet descended, three times the voice spoke, and three times Peter refused before the sheet was taken back into heaven.

Peter was deeply puzzled. He had no idea what this vision meant. He knew it had to mean something important, but what? Was God really telling him to throw away the food laws he had followed since childhood?

While he was still turning the vision over in his mind, the Spirit spoke to him directly: "Three men are looking for you. Get up and go downstairs. Do not hesitate to go with them, for I have sent them" (10:19–20).

Peter went downstairs and found Cornelius' messengers at the door. They explained who had sent them and why. Peter invited them in and gave them lodging for the night.

The next morning, Peter set out with them for Caesarea. He brought along some Jewish Christians from Joppa as witnesses. Whatever was about to happen, Peter wanted others to see it with their own eyes.

CROSSING THE THRESHOLD

When Peter arrived at Cornelius' house, the centurion had gathered his relatives and close friends. This was not a private meeting. Cornelius had filled his home with people who needed to hear whatever Peter had come to say.

Cornelius met Peter at the door and fell at his feet in reverence. Peter immediately pulled him up. "Stand up," he said. "I am only a man myself" (10:26). Then Peter walked inside. For a devout Jew, stepping across the threshold of a Gentile home was a radical act. Everything Peter had been taught told him this was wrong. But God had shown him otherwise.

Peter addressed the room honestly. "You are well aware that it is against our law for a Jew to associate with or visit a Gentile," he said. "But God has shown me that I should not call anyone impure or unclean" (10:28).

Did you catch that? The vision was never really about food. It was about people. The animals on the sheet represented the Gentiles that Peter and every other Jewish believer had been trained to consider unclean, unfit for the family of God. God was telling Peter that the old divisions were over. What God has declared clean, no man has the right to call unclean.

Cornelius told Peter about his own vision, the angel, and the instructions he had received. Then he said something beautiful: "Now we are all here in the presence of God to listen to everything the Lord has commanded you to tell us" (10:33). A room full of Gentiles was sitting at attention, ready to hear the word of God from the mouth of a Jewish fisherman. The wall was already cracking.

GOD SHOWS NO FAVORITISM

Peter opened his mouth and spoke words that shook the foundations of everything he had been raised to believe.

"I now realize how true it is that God does not show favoritism but accepts from every nation the one who fears him and does what is right" (10:34–35).

This was an earthquake statement. Peter, a lifelong Jew who had always believed that God's saving work was centered on Israel, was now standing in a Roman officer's living room declaring that God's arms were open to every nation. Not just to Jews. Not just to those who followed the law of Moses. To everyone who fears God and does what is right, regardless of their ethnicity, nationality, or background.

Then Peter preached Jesus. He told them about Jesus' baptism, his anointing with the Holy Spirit, and his ministry of doing good and healing all who were under the power of the devil. He told them how the leaders in Jerusalem had killed Jesus by nailing him to a cross. He told them that God raised him from the dead on the third day and that the apostles had eaten and drank with the risen Lord. He declared that Jesus had been appointed by God as the judge of the living and the dead, and that everyone who believes in him receives forgiveness of sins through his name (10:36–43).

This was the same gospel Peter had preached at Pentecost and at the temple after the lame man's healing. The message had not changed. But the audience had changed dramatically. For the first time, a Jewish apostle was preaching the full gospel to a room full of Gentiles.

THE SPIRIT FALLS

Peter never got to finish his sermon. "While Peter was still speaking these words, the Holy Spirit came on all who heard the message" (10:44). The Jewish Christians who had come with Peter from Joppa were astonished. The gift of the Holy Spirit had been poured out on Gentiles. They heard them speaking in tongues and praising God, the same miraculous signs that had accompanied the Spirit's arrival at Pentecost (10:45–46).

This was the moment that changed everything. The Spirit of God did not wait for Peter to issue an invitation or wait for the Gentiles to be circumcised or follow the dietary laws. He fell on them while Peter was still talking. God himself settled the question. If he was willing to give the Holy Spirit to uncircumcised Gentiles, then no human being had the right to shut them out.

Peter understood immediately. "Surely no one can stand in the way of their being baptized with water," he said. "They have received the Holy Spirit just as we have" (10:47). He ordered that Cornelius and his household be immersed in the name of Jesus Christ. They were welcomed fully into the people of God, not as second-class members who first had to become Jews but as Gentiles who believed in Jesus and received the same Spirit as every other believer.

It is important to notice what happened and what it meant. The Spirit's miraculous arrival on the Gentiles was not the norm for how people entered the church. It was an exceptional, unrepeatable sign designed to convince the Jewish believers that God had accepted these Gentiles. The Spirit fell before baptism in this case specifically so that no one could argue against their inclusion. It was God's way of saying, "I have made this decision. Now act on it."

And Peter did. He stayed with Cornelius for several days, sharing meals and fellowship with Gentiles for the first time in his life. The wall was down.

TROUBLE IN JERUSALEM

News travels fast when something scandalous happens, and word reached Jerusalem before Peter did. When he arrived, the Jewish believers confronted him immediately. "You went into the house of uncircumcised men and ate with them," they said (11:3). To them, this was a serious violation of everything they had been taught.

Peter didn't argue. He told them the whole story, step by step. The vision of the sheet. The voice that said, "Do not call anything impure that God has made clean." The Spirit's instruction to go with Cornelius' messengers without hesitation. The angel who had appeared to Cornelius. And then the decisive moment: the Spirit falling on the Gentiles while Peter was still speaking.

"I remembered what the Lord had said," Peter told them. "'John baptized with water, but you will be baptized with the Holy Spirit.' So if God gave them the same gift he gave us who believed in the Lord Jesus Christ, who was I to think that I could stand in God's way?" (11:16–17).

That last question is the key. Who was Peter, or anyone else, to oppose what God had clearly done? If the Spirit of God had fallen on these Gentiles, then God had accepted them. And if God had accepted them, then his people had no choice but to do the same.

The objections stopped. Luke tells us that when the Christians in Jerusalem heard this, they had no further objections and praised God, saying, "So then, even to Gentiles God has granted repentance that leads to life" (11:18).

It was the most important theological conclusion the early church ever reached. The gospel was not for Jews alone. It was for the whole world.

WHAT THIS MEANS FOR US

First, God's people sometimes need to unlearn things before they can move forward. Peter was not sinning by keeping the dietary laws. He had been faithful to what God had commanded under the old covenant. But a new era had arrived, and God was expanding his family in ways Peter had not expected. Growth sometimes means letting go of assumptions you have held your entire life and trusting that God knows what he is doing.

Second, the gospel does not belong to any one group. Peter's statement that "God does not show favoritism" is one of the most radical truths in the entire Bible. No nation, race, culture, or social class has a monopoly on God's grace. The same Jesus who died for the sins of Israel died for the sins of every person on earth. If someone fears God and seeks to do what is right, the door is open, no matter where they come from.

Third, God's actions settle arguments that human debates cannot. The Jerusalem believers could have argued about the Gentile question for years. But God settled it by pouring out the Spirit on Cornelius' household before anyone had a chance to object. When God acts, the only appropriate response is to follow.

Fourth, obedience sometimes means going where you are uncomfortable. Peter did not want to go to a Gentile house. Everything in his upbringing resisted it. But the Spirit told him to go, and he went. Some of the most important things God will ask you to do are things that feel uncomfortable, unfamiliar, or even wrong by the standards you grew up with. Trust the voice of the Spirit more than the voice of your comfort zone.

TALKING POINTS

1. **Peter's vision was about animals, but its real meaning was about people.** Why do you think God used such an indirect method to teach Peter this lesson? What might Peter have missed if God had simply told him, "Go to Cornelius"?

2. **Peter said, "God does not show favoritism."** What are some ways that people today still show favoritism based on race, nationality, or social status? How should this truth change the way we treat people who are different from us?

3. **The Spirit fell on Cornelius' household before they were baptized.** Why do you think God did it in that order instead of the normal pattern? What was he trying to prove, and to whom?

4. **When Peter told the Jerusalem church what had happened, they stopped objecting and praised God.** What does it look like to accept something you were initially opposed to because you recognize that God is behind it?

5. **Peter had to unlearn a lifetime of assumptions about clean and unclean people.** What assumptions or habits might Christians today need to unlearn in order to follow God more faithfully?

The wall between Jew and Gentile was down. The Spirit had been poured out on people from every nation. The church was no longer a Jewish sect. It was becoming what Jesus had always intended: a worldwide family united by faith in his name.

But as the gospel spread further from Jerusalem, a new question was forming. Just how far would this openness go? And would everyone in the church agree about the answer?

Turn the page.

7

INTO THE UNKNOWN

H. Rider Haggard's *King Solomon's Mines* begins when an experienced retired hunter named Allan Quatermain is asked to lead an expedition into the unexplored interior of Africa. The mission is dangerous. No European has ever crossed the desert that stands between them and the legendary diamond mines of King Solomon. The last man who tried left behind nothing but a scrawled map drawn in his own blood.

Quatermain knows the odds. He has every reason to say no. But he agrees to go anyway, and together with two companions he sets out into territory where no one can predict what will happen next. They nearly die of thirst in the desert. They are captured by a hostile king. They face treachery, battle, and starvation. At every turn, something threatens to end the expedition before it reaches its goal.

But they keep going. And what they find on the other side of the desert changes everything.

Acts 12–14 tells a story with the same shape. The church in Antioch, under the direction of the Holy Spirit, sends Barnabas and Saul out on a journey into territory where the gospel has never been preached. No one knows what they will find. The road ahead holds sorcerers, hostile crowds, furious mobs, and stones aimed at their heads. At one point, Paul is left for dead outside a city wall.

But before any of that begins, Luke shows us what was happening back in Jerusalem, where the church was about to lose one of its pillars and nearly lose another.

THE SWORD AND THE ANGEL

King Herod Agrippa I, grandson of the Herod who tried to kill the infant Jesus, decided to attack the church. He had James, the brother of John, executed with the sword (12:2). Luke records this in a single sentence with no additional detail. One of Jesus' closest disciples—one of the three who had been with him on the Mount of Transfiguration—was dead. Just like that.

When Herod saw that killing James pleased the Jewish leaders, he arrested Peter too. It was Passover season, and Herod intended to put Peter on public trial after the festival. He assigned four squads of four soldiers each to guard the apostle, sixteen men in total. Peter was chained between two soldiers, with sentries at the door. Herod was taking no chances.

But the church was taking action of its own kind. While Peter sat in chains, the Christians gathered in the house of Mary, the mother of John Mark, and prayed. Earnestly. Constantly. Through the night.

The very night before Herod planned to bring Peter out for trial, an angel of the Lord appeared in the cell. A light shone in the darkness. The angel struck Peter on the side to wake him and said, "Quick, get up!" The chains fell off Peter's wrists. "Put on your clothes and sandals," the angel told him. "Wrap your cloak around you and follow me" (12:7–8).

Peter obeyed, but he thought he was dreaming. He followed the angel past the first guard, past the second guard, and through the iron gate that led into the city. The gate opened by itself. They walked down one street, and the angel vanished.

Peter stood alone in the cool night air, free. "Now I know without a doubt," he said, "that the Lord has sent his angel and rescued me from Herod's grasp" (12:11).

He went straight to Mary's house. When he knocked on the outer door, a servant girl named Rhoda came to answer. She recognized Peter's voice and was so overjoyed that she forgot to open the door. She ran back inside shouting, "Peter is at the door!" The others told her she was out of her mind. Meanwhile, Peter kept knocking.

When they finally opened the door and saw him standing there, they were astonished. God had answered the very prayer they had been praying all night, and they could hardly believe it.

Peter told them to report what had happened to James, the brother of Jesus, who was becoming a leader in the Jerusalem church. Then Peter left and went to another place. When morning came and Herod's soldiers discovered the empty cell, the king was furious. He had the guards executed and left Jerusalem for Caesarea.

A KING WHO TOOK GOD'S GLORY

In Caesarea, Herod accepted flattery that no human should accept. During a public appearance in his royal robes, the crowd shouted, "This is the voice of a god, not of a man!" (12:22). Herod soaked it in. He did not give glory to God.

Immediately, an angel of the Lord struck him down. He was eaten by worms and died (12:23).

The contrast could not be sharper. An angel rescued Peter from prison. An angel struck Herod dead. God delivered his servant and destroyed the tyrant. The king who claimed divine honor was consumed, while the church he tried to crush kept growing.

Luke closes this section with a quiet but powerful summary: "But the word of God increased and multiplied" (12:24). Herod was gone. The gospel was not.

SET APART FOR THE WORK

The scene shifts to Antioch, the first predominantly Gentile church and the launching pad for what comes next. Luke introduces the leadership there: Barnabas, Simeon called Niger, Lucius of Cyrene, Manaen (who had been raised alongside Herod the tetrarch), and Saul. The diversity of this group is striking. A Jewish Levite from Cyprus. Two men from Africa. A man with connections to the royal court. A former Pharisee from Tarsus. The church at Antioch did not look like any single culture or background. It looked like the kingdom of God.

While they were worshiping and fasting, the Holy Spirit spoke: "Set apart for me Barnabas and Saul for the work to which I have called them" (13:2). The church fasted, prayed, laid hands on the two men, and sent them off.

Notice who was doing the sending. Luke says the church sent them (13:3), but he also says they were "sent out by the

Holy Spirit" (13:4). Both were true. The Spirit initiated the mission. The church confirmed and supported it. This was not a human strategy session. It was a divine commission, carried out through a community that was listening for God's voice.

Barnabas and Saul, accompanied by John Mark as their assistant, sailed to the island of Cyprus. The first planned missionary journey in church history had begun.

A SORCERER AND A GOVERNOR

On Cyprus, they made their way across the island to the city of Paphos, the seat of Roman government. There they encountered two very different men.

The first was a Jewish sorcerer and false prophet named Bar-Jesus, also called Elymas. He had attached himself to the Roman governor, Sergius Paulus, and had been using his dark arts to maintain influence over him. When Sergius Paulus invited Barnabas and Saul to come and explain the word of God, Elymas tried to interfere. He did everything he could to turn the governor away from the faith (13:8).

Saul, now called Paul for the first time in Luke's narrative, looked straight at the sorcerer and said, "You are a child of the devil and an enemy of everything that is right! Will you never stop perverting the straight paths of the Lord? Now the hand of the Lord is against you. You are going to be blind for a time" (13:10–11). Immediately, a dark mist fell over Elymas, and he stumbled around groping for someone to lead him by the hand.

When the governor saw what had happened, he believed, astonished at the teaching about the Lord (13:12).

The first stop on the first missionary journey was a head-on collision with the powers of darkness, and the power of the Holy Spirit won decisively.

A SERMON IN A SYNAGOGUE

From Cyprus, Paul and his companions sailed north to the mainland and traveled inland to Pisidian Antioch. On the Sabbath, they entered the synagogue. When the leaders invited them to speak, Paul stood up and delivered a sermon that covered the entire sweep of Israel's history: God's choice of Abraham, the exodus from Egypt, the wilderness years, the judges, King Saul, and then King David, the man after God's own heart.

All of it was building to one point. "From this man's descendants God has brought to Israel the Savior Jesus, as he promised" (13:23).

Paul told them how the people of Jerusalem and their rulers had failed to recognize Jesus and condemned him to death, fulfilling the very prophecies they read every Sabbath. But God raised him from the dead, and he appeared to many witnesses over many days. Through Jesus, Paul declared, forgiveness of sins is available. Everyone who believes in him is made right with God (13:38–39).

The response was electric. Many Jews and God-fearing Gentiles followed Paul and Barnabas, eager to hear more. The next Sabbath, nearly the whole city gathered to hear the word of the Lord. But when the Jewish leaders saw the crowds, they were filled with jealousy and began to contradict Paul.

Paul and Barnabas answered boldly: "We had to speak

the word of God to you first. Since you reject it and do not consider yourselves worthy of eternal life, we now turn to the Gentiles. For this is what the Lord has commanded us: 'I have made you a light for the Gentiles, that you may bring salvation to the ends of the earth'" (13:46–47).

The Gentiles in the crowd were thrilled. Many believed. But the Jewish leaders stirred up opposition and drove Paul and Barnabas out of the city. The missionaries shook the dust from their feet and moved on.

MISTAKEN FOR GODS, THEN STONED

In Iconium, the pattern repeated: successful preaching, a divided city, and eventually a plot to stone them. Paul and Barnabas fled south to the rural town of Lystra.

There, Paul healed a man who had been lame from birth, a man who had never taken a single step. When the crowd saw the miracle, they erupted with excitement. But they completely misunderstood what had happened. "The gods have come down to us in human form!" they shouted in their local dialect (14:11). They called Barnabas Zeus and Paul Hermes, and the local priest of Zeus brought bulls and wreaths to the city gates, preparing to offer sacrifices to them.

Paul and Barnabas were horrified. They tore their clothes and rushed into the crowd, shouting, "Friends, why are you doing this? We are only human, like you! We are bringing you good news, telling you to turn from these worthless things to the living God, who made the heavens and the earth and the sea and everything in them" (14:15). Even with this plea, they could barely stop the crowd from offering the sacrifice.

Then, in one of the most jarring reversals in the entire book, Jews arrived from Antioch and Iconium, turned the crowd against Paul, and stoned him. They dragged his body outside the city and left him for dead (14:19).

But the disciples gathered around him, and Paul got up. He walked back into the city. The next day, he and Barnabas left for Derbe and kept preaching.

Think about that. One moment the crowd wanted to worship Paul as a god. The next moment they were throwing rocks at his head. And the moment after that, Paul was back on his feet, heading to the next town. The mission did not stop. It could not be stopped.

THE ROAD HOME

After preaching in Derbe, Paul and Barnabas did something remarkable. Instead of taking the shorter route home, they retraced their steps through Lystra, Iconium, and Pisidian Antioch, the very cities where they had been persecuted. They went back to strengthen the young Christians and to deliver a message that would have carried enormous weight coming from men covered in scars: "We must go through many hardships to enter the kingdom of God" (14:22).

They appointed elders in every church. They prayed and fasted with the believers. They entrusted each congregation to the Lord in whom they had believed. Then they made their way back to Antioch, the church that had sent them.

When they arrived, they gathered the whole church together and reported everything God had done through them, and how he had opened the door of faith to the Gentiles (14:27).

The first missionary journey was complete. The gospel had reached new shores. Churches had been planted in hostile territory. Elders had been appointed. And the door to the Gentile world was now standing wide open.

WHAT THIS MEANS FOR US

First, prayer matters even when the situation looks impossible. Peter was in a maximum-security prison, chained to soldiers, with execution scheduled for the morning. The church had no political power, no legal strategy, and no rescue plan. They had prayer. And prayer was enough. God answered in a way none of them expected.

Second, the mission belongs to the Holy Spirit, not to us. The church at Antioch did not invent the idea of sending missionaries. The Spirit initiated it. The church's role was to listen, confirm, and support. When we treat the work of the gospel as our project to manage, we get it backward. The mission starts with God. Our job is to follow.

Third, opposition is not a sign that you are in the wrong place. Paul and Barnabas were opposed in nearly every city they entered. They were expelled, plotted against, and stoned. But they kept going, and churches were planted in every one of those hostile cities. Resistance from the world does not mean God has abandoned you. It may mean the gospel is doing exactly what it is supposed to do.

Fourth, faithfulness means going back. Paul and Barnabas could have gone straight home after being stoned. Instead, they went back through the places that had hurt them in order to strengthen the people they had led to faith. Faithfulness is not just about starting well. It is about returning, encouraging, and building up what God has begun, even when it costs you.

TALKING POINTS

1. **James was killed and Peter was rescued. Both were faithful apostles, yet their outcomes were very different.** How do you make sense of the fact that God sometimes delivers his people from danger and sometimes does not? What does this teach us about trusting God?

2. **The church at Antioch had leaders from wildly different backgrounds: Jewish, African, and politically connected.** Why do you think diversity in leadership matters for a church that is trying to reach the whole world?

3. **In Lystra, the crowd wanted to worship Paul and Barnabas as gods one moment and stoned Paul the next.** What does this tell us about the fickleness of public opinion? How should Christians respond when people's approval shifts quickly?

4. **Paul told the young churches that "we must go through many hardships to enter the kingdom of God."** Why do you think he made suffering part of the message instead of hiding it? How would you respond if someone told you that following Jesus would be hard?

5. **After being stoned and left for dead, Paul got up and went to the next city.** Where do you think that kind of resilience comes from? What would it take for you to keep going after a devastating setback?

The door of faith was open to the Gentiles, and churches were springing up across the Roman world. But not everyone was happy about how easy it was for Gentiles to get in. A group of Jewish believers was about to insist that Gentile converts must follow the law of Moses before they could truly belong. The church was heading for its biggest internal debate yet.

Turn the page.

8

THE BIGGEST QUESTION

Have you ever been told that you had to change who you are before you could belong? Maybe a group at school said you could sit with them at lunch, but only if you dressed a certain way or stopped hanging out with certain people. Maybe a team said you could join, but only if you dropped everything else you were doing. Or maybe you watched someone get shut out of a group because they didn't meet an unwritten list of requirements that nobody told them about until it was too late.

It's one of the most painful experiences there is: being told that who you are isn't enough. That you need to become someone else before you're welcome.

The early church faced this exact question, and everything hung on the answer. Gentiles were flooding into the faith. In city after city, people who had never been part of Israel—who had never followed the law of Moses, who had never been circumcised—were believing in Jesus and being baptized. The door of faith had been flung open, and people were streaming through it.

But now some Jewish believers were standing at that door with their arms crossed, saying, "Not so fast." They insisted that

Gentile converts had to be circumcised and follow the entire law of Moses before they could truly be saved. In other words, Gentiles had to become Jews before they could become Christians.

The answer to this question would determine the future of the church. If the answer was yes, Christianity would remain a branch of Judaism, and the gospel would be chained to a set of rituals that God had never intended for the nations. If the answer was no, the church would become what God always planned: a family drawn from every nation on earth, united by faith in Jesus alone.

The church gathered in Jerusalem to settle it.

TROUBLE FROM JUDEA

The crisis began when certain men came down from Judea to the church in Antioch and started teaching the Gentile believers, "Unless you are circumcised according to the custom prescribed by Moses, you cannot be saved" (15:1).

This was not a minor theological disagreement. These men were saying that faith in Jesus was not enough. They were adding a requirement to the gospel that Jesus himself had never imposed and that the Holy Spirit had already shown to be unnecessary. Worse, they had come without the authorization of the Jerusalem church (15:24). They were acting on their own authority, stirring up confusion and fear among Christians who had been happily following Jesus without any thought of becoming Jewish converts.

Paul and Barnabas pushed back immediately. A sharp dispute broke out. The church at Antioch decided to send Paul, Barnabas, and some other believers to Jerusalem to bring the question before the apostles and elders. This was too important for one congregation to settle on its own. The whole church needed to weigh in.

As they traveled south through Phoenicia and Samaria, Paul and Barnabas told the Christians in those regions how Gentiles had been turning to God. The news brought great joy everywhere they went (15:3). But when they arrived in Jerusalem and reported what God had done, a group of believers who belonged to the party of the Pharisees stood up and declared, "The Gentiles must be circumcised and required to keep the law of Moses" (15:5).

The battle lines were drawn. The apostles and elders gathered to consider the matter. And what followed was one of the most important debates in the history of the church.

PETER SPEAKS FROM EXPERIENCE

After much discussion, Peter stood up. He had been quiet, but now he had something to say that no one else in the room could say, because no one else had been where he had been.

"Brothers," he said, "you know that some time ago God made a choice among you that the Gentiles might hear from my lips the message of the gospel and believe" (15:7). Peter was pointing back to the house of Cornelius, where God had poured out the Holy Spirit on uncircumcised Gentiles while Peter was still preaching. The entire room knew the story. It had been told and retold. God himself had settled this question before anyone had asked it.

"God, who knows the heart," Peter continued, "showed that he accepted them by giving the Holy Spirit to them, just as he did to us. He did not discriminate between us and them, for he purified their hearts by faith" (15:8–9).

Then Peter asked a question that silenced the room. "Now then, why do you try to test God by putting on the necks of Gentile disciples a yoke that neither we nor our ancestors have been able to bear?" (15:10).

Peter was being blunt. The law of Moses, as an entire system of commands and rituals, was a burden that Israel itself had never managed to carry faithfully. Generation after generation had stumbled under its weight. So how could anyone demand that Gentiles shoulder a load that Jews themselves had never successfully borne?

Peter finished with a statement that cut to the heart of the gospel: "We believe it is through the grace of the Lord Jesus that we are saved, just as they are" (15:11).

Did you catch the order of that sentence? Peter did not say, "They are saved the same way we are." He said, "*We* are saved the same way *they* are." Even Jewish believers were not saved by keeping the law. They were saved by grace, through faith in Jesus, exactly like the Gentiles. The playing field was level. No one had an advantage. No one needed an extra step. Grace was the ground everyone stood on.

PAUL AND BARNABAS ADD THEIR EVIDENCE

After Peter finished, the entire assembly fell silent. Then Barnabas and Paul stood up and told about the miraculous signs and wonders God had done among the Gentiles through them (15:12). They did not argue theology. They simply described what God had been doing: healing the sick, casting out demons, converting entire communities, planting churches. If God was working this powerfully among uncircumcised Gentiles, who could say he had not accepted them?

The evidence was overwhelming. God's own actions had answered the question before the council ever met.

JAMES TURNS TO SCRIPTURE

When Paul and Barnabas finished, James spoke. This was James, the brother of Jesus, who had become a key leader of the Jerusalem church. He had listened to Peter's testimony and to the reports of Paul and Barnabas. Now he brought the discussion to its foundation: the Scriptures.

"Brothers, listen to me," he said. "Simon has described to us how God first intervened to choose a people for his name from the Gentiles" (15:13–14). Then James quoted from the prophet Amos: "After this I will return and rebuild David's fallen tent. Its ruins I will rebuild, and I will restore it, that the rest of mankind may seek the Lord, even all the Gentiles who bear my name, says the Lord, who does these things, things known from long ago."

James' point was crucial. The inclusion of Gentiles was not a break from God's plan. It was the fulfillment of God's plan. The prophets had always said that when God restored the kingdom of David, the nations would come streaming in. That was exactly what was happening. Gentiles were seeking the Lord, not because the church had gone off-script, but because God was doing what he had promised to do all along.

Based on all of this—Peter's experience, the evidence of God's work among the Gentiles, and the witness of Scripture—

James gave his judgment. "It is my judgment, therefore, that we should not make it difficult for the Gentiles who are turning to God" (15:19).

The demand for circumcision was rejected. Gentiles did not need to become Jews. They were welcomed as Gentiles, saved by grace through faith in Jesus, just as Peter had said.

FOUR THINGS TO AVOID

James did, however, propose that the council write to the Gentile believers asking them to avoid four specific practices: things polluted by idols, sexual immorality, meat from strangled animals, and blood (15:20).

These were not conditions for salvation. The council had just established that salvation came through grace, not through law-keeping. So what were these four requirements about?

All four were deeply connected to pagan temple worship. In the cities where Gentile Christians lived, the temples of false gods were the center of social life. Feasts held in those temples involved meat sacrificed to idols, ritual sexual immorality, and the consumption of blood, which was associated with pagan rituals. These practices defined the world the Gentiles had just left behind. James was telling Gentile believers to make a clean break from the worship of false gods. Following Jesus meant leaving the temple of Zeus and Aphrodite behind for good.

These restrictions also made it possible for Jewish and Gentile believers to share fellowship together. Jewish Christians would have found it deeply offensive to sit at a table with someone who had just come from a pagan feast or who was still participating in practices tied to idol worship. The four requirements cleared the path for genuine unity between the two groups, not by forcing Gentiles to become Jews, but by asking them to abandon the practices of their old, pagan life.

THE LETTER

The whole church, along with the apostles and elders, agreed to send a letter to the Gentile believers in Antioch, Syria, and Cilicia. They chose two respected men, Judas called Barsabbas and Silas, to carry the letter and deliver it in person alongside Paul and Barnabas.

The letter began by acknowledging that the men who had caused the trouble in Antioch had gone out without authorization from Jerusalem (15:24). The church disowned their teaching. Then it stated the council's decision in language that should take your breath away:

"It seemed good to the Holy Spirit and to us not to burden you with anything beyond the following requirements" (15:28).

The Holy Spirit and us. The council believed that the Spirit of God had guided their discussion and confirmed their conclusion. This was not a human committee making a political compromise. It was the people of God, led by the Spirit of God, arriving at the truth of God.

The letter listed the four requirements and closed with a simple encouragement: "You will do well to avoid these things. Farewell" (15:29).

JOY IN ANTIOCH

When the delegation arrived in Antioch and read the letter to the gathered church, the response was immediate. "The people read it and were glad for its encouraging message" (15:31). Judas and Silas, who were both prophets, stayed for a time to encourage and strengthen the believers.

The crisis was over. The gospel was free. Gentiles could follow Jesus as Gentiles. Jews could follow Jesus as Jews. And both were saved the same way: through the grace of the Lord Jesus Christ.

The church had faced the biggest question of its young life and, guided by the Spirit, had answered it correctly. What could have torn the movement apart instead made it stronger. What could have chained the gospel to one nation instead set it free for every nation on earth.

WHAT THIS MEANS FOR US

First, the gospel is the same for everyone. There is not one way to be saved for one group and a different way for another. Peter declared that Jews and Gentiles alike are saved through the grace of the Lord Jesus. No cultural background, ethnic identity, or religious tradition adds anything to what Jesus has already done. Grace is the only ground.

Second, God's actions should shape our theology, not the other way around. Peter pointed to what God had done among the Gentiles. Paul and Barnabas described the signs and wonders they had witnessed. James showed that Scripture confirmed the same conclusion. When God is clearly at work, the faithful response is not to argue with him but to follow where he leads.

Third, unity sometimes requires sacrifice on both sides. The council did not ask Gentiles to become Jews. But it did ask them to abandon practices tied to their old pagan life. Unity in the church is not achieved by one side dominating the other. It is achieved when everyone is willing to lay down what needs to go for the sake of fellowship with God and with one another.

Fourth, good leaders listen before they decide. The council heard from Peter, Paul, Barnabas, and James. They listened to experience, evidence, and Scripture. They debated. They considered. And only then did they reach a conclusion. The best decisions in the church are not made by one person in a hurry. They are made by godly people who take the time to hear each other and seek the mind of the Spirit together.

TALKING POINTS

1. **Peter said the law of Moses was "a yoke that neither we nor our ancestors have been able to bear."** What do you think he meant by that? How does the gospel offer something different from a list of rules that people constantly fail to keep?

2. **The men who caused the crisis had come from Jerusalem without authorization.** Why is it dangerous when people teach things on their own authority rather than with the backing of the larger community of believers?

3. **James based his decision on what God had done (through Peter, Paul, and Barnabas) and on what God had said (through the prophet Amos).** Why is it important to look at both experience and Scripture when making important decisions? What happens when you rely on only one of those?

4. **The four requirements given to Gentile believers were all connected to pagan temple practices.** Why do you think it was important for new believers to make a clean break from

their old way of worship? Are there things in our culture today that followers of Jesus should avoid for similar reasons?

5. The letter said the decision "seemed good to the Holy Spirit and to us." What does it look like for a group of Christians to seek the guidance of the Holy Spirit when making decisions together? How can you tell the difference between the Spirit's leading and just going along with what the majority wants?

The question had been answered. The gospel was for every nation, and no one had to become someone else to receive it. Paul was now free to take the message of Jesus to the far reaches of the Roman Empire without anyone demanding that his converts first pass through the gate of Jewish law.

But first, a painful parting. Paul and Barnabas, the team that had braved sorcerers and stonings together, were about to go their separate ways.

Turn the page.

9

FARTHER THAN BEFORE

Virgil's *The Aeneid* tells the story of a man who cannot stop moving. After the fall of Troy, a warrior named Aeneas gathers the survivors and sets sail across the Mediterranean Sea. He does not choose this journey. The gods have given him a mission: carry the remnants of his civilization to a new homeland in Italy and lay the foundations for what will become the greatest empire the world has ever seen. Aeneas has no map for this. He only has a command and a promise.

At every port, something goes wrong. Storms scatter his fleet. A queen tries to keep him from leaving. Friends die. Enemies attack. Local rulers misunderstand his mission. Over and over, Aeneas is tempted to settle down, give up, or turn back. But the divine command keeps pushing him forward, and each stop along the way, no matter how painful, brings him closer to the destination he was born to reach.

Paul's second missionary journey has the same shape. Armed with nothing but the Holy Spirit and the message of a risen King, Paul crossed the sea into Europe for the first time and carried the gospel to cities that had never heard it. He was misunderstood, arrested, beaten, mocked, and dragged before courts. At every stop, something unexpected happened. And at every stop, the gospel took root.

A PAINFUL PARTING

Before the journey began, a friendship ended. Paul suggested to Barnabas that they revisit the churches they had planted on their first trip. Barnabas agreed but wanted to bring John Mark along. Paul refused. John Mark had abandoned them during the first journey, turning back when the work got hard (13:13), and Paul was not willing to take that risk again.

The disagreement was sharp. Luke uses a strong word: it was so heated that Paul and Barnabas "parted company" (15:39). The two men who had faced sorcerers and stonings side by side, who had stood together before the Jerusalem Council, could not agree on this. Barnabas took John Mark and sailed to Cyprus. Paul chose Silas and headed north through Syria and Cilicia, strengthening the churches along the way.

It is worth pausing here, because Luke does not hide this. Two Spirit-filled men disagreed so deeply that they split up. The Bible does not pretend that Christians always get along. But notice what God did with the mess. Instead of one team going out, now there were two. The gospel went to more places, not fewer. God can use even our conflicts to advance his purposes.

TIMOTHY JOINS THE TEAM

In Lystra, Paul found a young disciple named Timothy. His mother was a Jewish believer, but his father was a Greek. The believers in Lystra and Iconium spoke highly of him. Paul wanted Timothy to join the team, so he had him circumcised before they left (16:3).

Wait. Didn't the Jerusalem Council just say that circumcision was not required for Gentile believers? Yes. But Timothy was half-Jewish, and Paul knew they would be preaching in synagogues where an uncircumcised man with a Jewish mother would be a scandal. This was not about salvation. It was about removing an unnecessary obstacle to the mission. Paul was willing to adapt on matters that did not compromise the gospel for the sake of reaching more people.

BLOCKED BY THE SPIRIT

What happened next is one of the most unusual passages in Acts. Paul and his companions traveled through the region of Phrygia and Galatia, delivering the Jerusalem Council's decisions to the churches. But when they tried to preach in the province of Asia, the Holy Spirit stopped them. They headed north toward Bithynia, and the Spirit of Jesus would not allow them to go there either (16:6–7).

Imagine how confusing this must have been. They had been commissioned to preach the gospel. They were ready. They were willing. And the Spirit kept saying no. Not here. Not there. Not yet.

They ended up in Troas, a port city on the western coast, essentially at the edge of the continent. And there, during the night, Paul had a vision. A man from Macedonia stood before him, pleading, "Come over to Macedonia and help us!" (16:9).

Paul understood immediately. God was not blocking the mission. He was redirecting it. The gospel was about to cross the sea into Europe for the first time.

THREE CONVERSIONS IN PHILIPPI

Paul and his companions sailed from Troas to the Roman colony of Philippi, the leading city of the district of Macedonia. There was no synagogue in the city, so on the Sabbath they went outside the city gate to a riverbank where a group of women had gathered for prayer.

One of those women was Lydia, a dealer in expensive purple cloth from the city of Thyatira. Luke tells us that "the Lord opened her heart to respond to Paul's message" (16:14). She and her entire household were baptized, and she insisted that Paul and his companions stay at her home. Lydia became the first European convert and the host of the first church in Philippi.

But the visit took a dark turn. A slave girl who was possessed by an evil spirit followed Paul and his companions for days, shouting, "These men are servants of the Most High God, who are telling you the way to be saved!" (16:17). Eventually Paul turned and commanded the spirit to leave her in the name of Jesus Christ. It came out immediately.

The girl's owners were furious. She had been making them money as a fortune-teller, and now their source of income was gone. They dragged Paul and Silas before the city magistrates, accusing them of causing trouble and promoting customs unlawful for Romans. The crowd joined in, and the magistrates ordered Paul and Silas stripped, beaten with rods, and thrown into the inner cell of the prison with their feet locked in stocks (16:22–24).

What Paul and Silas did next is one of the most remarkable scenes in all of Scripture. Around midnight, bleeding and aching in a dark cell, they began to pray and sing hymns to God. The other prisoners listened.

Suddenly a violent earthquake shook the prison. Every door flew open. Every chain came loose. The jailer woke up and saw the open doors. Assuming the prisoners had escaped, which would have meant his execution, he drew his sword to kill himself.

Paul shouted, "Don't harm yourself! We are all here!" (16:28).

The jailer rushed in, fell trembling before Paul and Silas, and asked the most important question of his life: "Sirs, what must I do to be saved?" (16:30).

"Believe in the Lord Jesus," they answered, "and you will be saved, you and your household" (16:31). They spoke the word of the Lord to him and everyone in his house. That same hour, in the middle of the night, the jailer washed their wounds, and he and his whole household were baptized. Then he brought them into his home and set a meal before them. He was filled with joy because he had come to believe in God (16:33–34).

The next morning the magistrates sent word to release them. Paul refused to slip away quietly. He and Silas were Roman citizens who had been publicly beaten and imprisoned without a trial. The magistrates were alarmed and came personally to escort them out, begging them to leave the city. Paul and Silas went to Lydia's house, encouraged the Christians, and moved on.

THESSALONICA AND BEREA

In Thessalonica, Paul went to the synagogue and for three Sabbaths reasoned from the Scriptures, explaining and proving that the Messiah had to suffer and rise from the dead. "This Jesus I am proclaiming to you is the Messiah," he declared (17:3).

Some Jews were persuaded, along with a large number of God-fearing Greeks and quite a few prominent women.

But the Jewish leaders who rejected the message were jealous. They rounded up a mob and started a riot. Unable to find Paul, they dragged a believer named Jason before the city officials, shouting, "These men who have turned the world upside down have come here too! They are all defying Caesar's decrees, saying that there is another king, one called Jesus" (17:6–7).

The charge was explosive. In a Roman colony, claiming there was another king besides Caesar was treason. The officials made Jason post bond, and the believers sent Paul and Silas away by night to Berea.

In Berea, the response was different. Luke pays these people a rare compliment: they were "of more noble character than those in Thessalonica, for they received the message with great eagerness and examined the Scriptures every day to see if what Paul said was true" (17:11). Many believed, including prominent Greek women and men. But Jews from Thessalonica followed Paul to Berea and stirred up trouble there too. The believers quickly sent Paul to the coast, while Silas and Timothy stayed behind.

ATHENS: THE UNKNOWN GOD

Paul arrived in Athens alone, and what he saw disturbed him deeply. The city was full of idols. Statues and shrines to every god imaginable lined the streets. Paul went to the synagogue and also debated daily in the marketplace with whoever would listen. Some Epicurean and Stoic philosophers took an interest and brought him to the Areopagus, a council that met on a hill called Mars Hill, where they evaluated new ideas and teachings.

Standing before the most educated audience he had ever addressed, Paul delivered a masterpiece of cross-cultural preaching.

"People of Athens," he began, "I see that in every way you are very religious. For as I walked around and looked carefully at your objects of worship, I even found an altar with this inscription: TO AN UNKNOWN GOD. So you are ignorant of the very thing you worship, and this is what I am going to proclaim to you" (17:22–23).

Paul then described the God they did not know: the Creator of the world and everything in it, the Lord of heaven and earth, who does not live in temples built by human hands and is not served by human hands as if he needed anything. He made every nation from one man and determined where and when each would live, so that people would seek him and perhaps reach out for him and find him (17:24–27).

Then Paul drove to his conclusion. God had overlooked the times of ignorance, but now he commands all people everywhere to repent, because he has set a day when he will judge the world with justice by the man he has appointed. He has given proof of this to everyone by raising him from the dead (17:30–31).

At the mention of resurrection, the crowd split. Some sneered. Others said, "We want to hear you again on this subject." A few believed, including a member of the Areopagus named Dionysius and a woman named Damaris (17:32–34). Athens was not a sweeping success, but the seed was planted.

CORINTH: DO NOT BE AFRAID

From Athens, Paul traveled to Corinth, one of the largest and most morally bankrupt cities in the empire. There he met a Jewish couple named Aquila and Priscilla, who had been expelled from Rome along with all other Jews by the emperor Claudius. They were tentmakers by trade, and so was Paul, so he stayed with them and worked alongside them while preaching in the synagogue every Sabbath (18:1–4).

When the Jews in Corinth rejected his message and became abusive, Paul shook out his clothes and said, "Your blood is on your own heads! I am innocent. From now on I will go to the Gentiles" (18:6). He moved next door to the house of a God-fearing man named Titius Justus. Even the synagogue ruler, Crispus, believed in the Lord with his whole household, and many Corinthians heard the message, believed, and were baptized (18:8).

Paul must have been exhausted and discouraged. He had been beaten in Philippi, chased out of Thessalonica, driven from Berea, and mocked in Athens. One night the Lord spoke to him in a vision: "Do not be afraid. Keep on speaking, do not be silent. For I am with you, and no one is going to attack and harm you, because I have many people in this city" (18:9–10).

Those words kept Paul in Corinth for a year and a half, the longest he had stayed anywhere. When the Jews brought him before the Roman governor Gallio, accusing him of persuading people to worship God in unlawful ways, Gallio dismissed the case outright. He refused to judge matters of Jewish religious law. The Roman court had effectively declared the Christian movement innocent.

Paul eventually left Corinth, sailed across the sea, and returned to his home base, completing the second missionary journey (18:18–22). Behind him stretched a trail of new churches in Philippi, Thessalonica, Berea, and Corinth, communities that would receive some of the most important letters ever written.

WHAT THIS MEANS FOR US

First, God's direction sometimes comes through closed doors. Paul tried to go to Asia and Bithynia, and the Spirit said no. When God blocks your path, he is not punishing you. He is steering you. The closed door may be leading you to a Macedonian man standing on the other side of the sea.

Second, joy is possible in the worst circumstances. Paul and Silas sang hymns in a prison cell at midnight with open wounds on their backs. Joy like that does not come from comfortable conditions. It comes from a deep trust that God is still in control, even when everything around you says otherwise.

Third, different audiences need different approaches. Paul quoted Scripture in the synagogue, told the story of Jesus in Philippi, and used Greek philosophy in Athens. The message never changed, but the way he communicated it adapted to whoever was listening. Faithfulness to the gospel does not mean using the same words in every situation. It means finding the best way to help each person understand the truth.

Fourth, the Lord's presence is the ultimate encouragement. When Paul was ready to give up in Corinth, Jesus appeared and said, "I am with you." That promise did not remove the opposition. It gave Paul the courage to face it. The same promise belongs to every Christian today.

TALKING POINTS

1. **Paul and Barnabas had a sharp disagreement and split up.** Do you think either of them was wrong? What can we learn about handling conflict between Christians from the way this story is told?

2. **The Holy Spirit prevented Paul from going to Asia and Bithynia.** Have you ever had a plan that didn't work out, only to realize later that something better was waiting? How do you recognize God's redirection in your own life?

3. **Paul and Silas sang hymns in prison at midnight.** What do you think gave them the ability to worship in that situation? How is their response different from what most people would do?

4. **In Athens, Paul started his sermon by connecting with what the Athenians already believed before introducing Jesus.** Why is it important to understand someone's world before trying to share the gospel with them? How can you do this in your own conversations?

5. **Jesus told Paul, "I have many people in this city."** What does it mean that Jesus already knew who would believe before Paul even preached to them? How should this truth affect the way we think about sharing our faith?

The second missionary journey was over. Churches stretched across Macedonia and Achaia. The gospel had reached Europe. But Paul was not finished. A third journey was already forming in his mind, and it would take him back through familiar territory and into new storms.

Turn the page.

10

THE LONG GOODBYE

Soul Surfer is the true story of Bethany Hamilton, a thirteen-year-old competitive surfer from Hawaii who lost her left arm in a shark attack. One morning she was paddling in calm water with her best friend's family. The next moment, a fourteen-foot tiger shark bit through her board and took her arm just below the shoulder.

Everyone assumed her surfing days were over.

But Bethany refused to quit. Within weeks she was back in the ocean, learning to paddle with one arm, retraining her balance, and figuring out how to do what everyone said was impossible. She entered competitions. She wiped out. She got back on the board. She wiped out again. And she kept coming back until she was competing at the national level, against surfers with two arms, and winning.

The part of the film that stays with you is not the shark attack. It is the refusal to stop. No matter what hit her, Bethany kept getting back on the board.

That is Paul in Acts 18–20. During his third missionary journey, Paul spent nearly three years in the city of Ephesus, one of the largest and most spiritually hostile cities in the Roman Empire. He faced sorcerers, exorcists, a citywide riot, and constant Jewish opposition. But he never stopped preaching. And when it was finally time to leave, knowing that prison and suffering waited for him in Jerusalem, he gathered the elders of the Ephesian church and gave them one of the most emotional farewell speeches in the entire Bible.

This chapter is about a man who refused to quit, and the people he had to leave behind.

APOLLOS AND THE TWELVE IN EPHESUS

Before Paul arrived in Ephesus for his extended stay, two important episodes set the stage.

First, a brilliant Jewish teacher named Apollos showed up. He was from Alexandria in Egypt, was an eloquent speaker, and knew the Scriptures deeply. He taught about Jesus with accuracy and passion. But he had one gap in his understanding: he only knew about the baptism of John (18:25). Priscilla and Aquila, the couple Paul had met in Corinth, heard him speak and privately explained the way of God to him more fully (18:26). Apollos didn't resist. He learned. He grew. And he went on to become a powerful ally to the churches in Corinth, refuting opponents of the gospel with skill and fire.

Second, when Paul himself reached Ephesus, he found about twelve men who called themselves disciples but whose knowledge was even more limited than Apollos'. When Paul asked if they had received the Holy Spirit when they believed, they said they hadn't even heard that there was a Holy Spirit (19:2). They had only been baptized into John's baptism. Paul explained that John's baptism was meant to prepare people for the one who came after him, Jesus. When they heard this, they were baptized in the name of the Lord Jesus. Paul laid his hands on them, and the Holy Spirit came on them. They spoke in tongues and prophesied (19:5–6).

This was Ephesus' Pentecost. Just as the Spirit had fallen on the twelve apostles in Jerusalem, on the Samaritans, and on Cornelius' household, the Spirit now fell on these twelve men in the heart of pagan Asia. A new outpost of the kingdom had been established.

THREE YEARS IN EPHESUS

Paul threw himself into the work. For three months he spoke boldly in the synagogue, arguing and persuading people about the kingdom of God. When some Jews became hostile and spoke publicly against the Way, Paul withdrew from the synagogue and moved his daily discussions to the lecture hall of a man named Tyrannus (19:8–9). This went on for two years, until, as Luke puts it, "all the residents of Asia, both Jews and Greeks, heard the word of the Lord" (19:10).

God also performed extraordinary miracles through Paul. Handkerchiefs and aprons that had touched him were carried to the sick, and diseases left them and evil spirits came out (19:11–12). Ephesus was a city drenched in superstition and magic, and God was making it unmistakably clear that the power behind Paul's ministry was in a completely different category from anything the city had seen before.

THE NAME THAT CANNOT BE BORROWED

Some Jewish exorcists in Ephesus tried to cash in on what they had seen. They started invoking the name of Jesus over people with evil spirits, saying, "In the name of the Jesus whom Paul preaches, I command you to come out" (19:13). Seven sons of a man named Sceva were doing this regularly.

One day the evil spirit answered them back. "Jesus I know, and Paul I recognize, but who are you?" (19:15). Then the man with the demon jumped on all seven of them, overpowered them, and beat them so badly that they ran out of the house naked and bleeding.

The story spread through the entire city, and fear fell on everyone. The name of the Lord Jesus was held in high honor (19:17). Many Christians who had been secretly holding on to their old magical practices came forward, confessed what they had been doing, and publicly burned their scrolls of magic spells. Luke tells us the total value of those scrolls was fifty thousand pieces of silver, a staggering fortune (19:19).

Then comes one of the great summary statements in Acts: "In this way the word of the Lord spread widely and grew in power" (19:20). The gospel was winning. Not through politics or military force, but through the power of the name of Jesus proclaimed by faithful witnesses.

A RIOT IN THE STREETS

But the gospel's success created enemies. A silversmith named Demetrius, who made his living crafting miniature shrines of the goddess Artemis, saw his business drying up. Paul had been telling people throughout Asia that gods made by human hands are not gods at all, and people were listening. Sales were plummeting.

Demetrius gathered his fellow craftsmen and laid out the problem bluntly: "Not only is there a danger that our trade will lose its good name, but also that the temple of the great goddess Artemis will be discredited" (19:27). He framed it as a religious concern, but his real worry was money.

The crowd erupted. "Great is Artemis of the Ephesians!" they shouted, and the entire city was thrown into confusion. People rushed into the enormous outdoor theater, dragging two of Paul's companions with them. Paul wanted to go in and address the crowd, but his friends and even some local officials who were sympathetic to him begged him not to (19:30–31).

Inside the theater, the scene was chaos. Most of the people didn't even know why they were there (19:32). For two hours the crowd chanted, "Great is Artemis of the Ephesians!" until a city clerk finally managed to quiet them down. He pointed out that Paul and his companions had committed no crime. They had neither robbed temples nor blasphemed the goddess. If Demetrius had a legal complaint, there were courts for that. "As it is," the clerk warned, "we are in danger of being charged with rioting" (19:40). The crowd dispersed.

Once again, the Way had been declared innocent by a public official. And once again, the real troublemakers turned out to be the people who were opposing the gospel, not the people preaching it.

A YOUNG MAN FALLS

After the riot settled, Paul left Ephesus and traveled through Macedonia and Greece, encouraging the churches along the way. On his return trip, he stopped in Troas, where the believers gathered on the first day of the week to break bread together. Paul spoke to them long into the night because he was leaving the next day, and he kept talking until midnight (20:7).

A young man named Eutychus was sitting in an open window on the third floor. As Paul's sermon stretched on, Eutychus sank into a deep sleep. He fell from the window and was picked up dead (20:9).

Paul went downstairs, threw his arms around the young man, and said, "Don't be alarmed. He's alive!" (20:10). Eutychus was restored, and the believers were deeply comforted. Paul went back upstairs, broke bread with them, and kept talking until dawn.

It's a scene that would be almost funny if it weren't so serious. A young man literally dies from falling asleep during a sermon and is raised back to life. But for Luke, this small story carries the same message as the rest of Paul's journey: wherever Paul went, he brought the life and power of the risen Jesus. Even death could not have the final word.

THE FAREWELL AT MILETUS

Paul was in a hurry to reach Jerusalem by the day of Pentecost, so he bypassed Ephesus and sailed to the nearby port of Miletus. From there he sent word to the elders of the Ephesian church, asking them to come to him. When they arrived, Paul gave them his final instructions.

This speech is unlike anything else in Acts. It is not a sermon to outsiders. It is a farewell from a man who loved these people deeply and knew he would never see them again.

Paul began by reminding them of how he had lived among them. "You know," he said, "how I lived the whole time I was with you, from the first day I came into the province of Asia. I served the Lord with great humility and with tears and in the midst of severe testing" (20:18–19). He had not held anything back. He had taught them publicly and from house to house, declaring to both Jews and Greeks that they must turn to God in repentance and have faith in the Lord Jesus (20:20–21).

Then came the words that reveal the depth of Paul's courage. "And now, compelled by the Spirit, I am going to Jerusalem, not knowing what will happen to me there. I only know that in every city the Holy Spirit warns me that prison and hardships are facing me" (20:22–23).

He knew what was coming. The Spirit had told him plainly. And yet, "I consider my life worth nothing to me; my only aim is to finish the race and complete the task the Lord Jesus has given me, the task of testifying to the good news of God's grace" (20:24).

Paul then declared that he was "innocent of the blood of all of you" because he had not hesitated to proclaim to them "the whole will of God" (20:26–27). He had preached the full message, leaving nothing out, softening nothing, regardless of the consequences.

Then he turned from his own story to theirs. "Keep watch over yourselves and all the flock of which the Holy Spirit has made you overseers. Be shepherds of the church of God, which he bought with his own blood" (20:28). The church did not belong to Paul. It did not belong to the elders. It belonged to God, purchased at the price of the blood of his Son. Their job was to care for it, protect it, and feed it.

Paul warned them that after he left, "savage wolves" would come in among them, not sparing the flock. Even from among their own number, men would arise and distort the truth to draw away disciples after them (20:29–30). The danger was not only from outside enemies. It was from inside the church.

He pointed them to his own example. "I have not coveted anyone's silver or gold or clothing," he said. "You yourselves know that these hands of mine have supplied my own needs and the needs of my companions. In everything I did, I showed you that by this kind of hard work we must help the weak, remembering the words the Lord Jesus himself said: 'It is more blessed to give than to receive'" (20:33–35).

When he finished, Paul knelt down with all of them and prayed. Luke tells us they all wept. They embraced him and kissed him. What grieved them most was his statement that they would never see his face again (20:37–38).

Then they accompanied him to the ship.

WHAT THIS MEANS FOR US

First, the gospel confronts every form of spiritual darkness. In Ephesus, Paul faced sorcerers, fake exorcists, and an entire economy built on idol worship. The power of Jesus' name proved greater than all of it. No spiritual force, no cultural system, and no economic interest can stand against the word of the Lord when it is faithfully proclaimed.

Second, faithful leaders declare the whole truth, not just the popular parts. Paul told the Ephesian elders he had proclaimed "the whole will of God." He didn't skip the uncomfortable subjects or soften the hard truths. A good teacher tells people what they need to hear, not just what they want to hear.

Third, the church needs shepherds who watch and protect. Paul's warning about "savage wolves" was not paranoia. It was prophecy. False teachers have always been one of the greatest threats to the church, and they usually come from within. The church needs leaders who are alert, courageous, and willing to guard the truth even when it costs them.

Fourth, finishing well matters more than starting well. Paul's goal was not comfort. It was completion. "I consider my life worth nothing to me; my only aim is to finish the race." The Christian life is not a sprint. It is a marathon. What matters is not how fast you start but whether you cross the finish line.

TALKING POINTS

1. **The sons of Sceva tried to use the name of Jesus like a magic formula, and it backfired spectacularly.** What is the difference between genuinely relying on Jesus and simply using his name for your own purposes?

2. **The Ephesian riot started because the gospel was hurting Demetrius' business.** Can you think of situations today where the message of Jesus conflicts with someone's financial interests? How should Christians respond when the gospel is costly?

3. **Paul told the Ephesian elders he had "not hesitated to proclaim the whole will of God."** Why is it important to teach the full truth and not just the parts that are easy or

popular? What happens to a church that only hears comfortable messages?

4. Paul warned that "savage wolves" would come into the church after he left. What do you think these "wolves" look like in the church today? How can Christians recognize and guard against false teaching?

5. Paul said, "It is more blessed to give than to receive." This is the only saying of Jesus recorded in Acts that is not found in the four Gospels. Why do you think Paul chose to end his farewell speech with this particular teaching? What does it tell us about what matters most in the Christian life?

Paul boarded the ship and sailed south. Behind him, weeping friends stood on the shore at Miletus. Ahead of him, the Holy Spirit's warnings hung in the air like storm clouds: prison and hardships in every city.

Paul knew exactly what was coming. And he went anyway.

Turn the page.

11

ON TRIAL

Fyodor Dostoevsky's *Crime and Punishment* contains one of the most famous interrogation scenes in all of literature. A detective named Porfiry sits across from a young man named Raskolnikov, and the two of them talk. On the surface, the detective is asking routine questions. But beneath the surface, something far more interesting is happening. The detective already suspects the truth, and Raskolnikov knows it. With every conversation, the walls close in a little tighter. Every question is a test. Every answer reveals more than the suspect intends.

But here is what makes the scene unforgettable: the detective is not just trying to catch a criminal. He is trying to save one. Porfiry believes that if Raskolnikov can be forced to face the truth about himself, he might actually find redemption. The interrogation is not just about guilt. It is about what happens when a person finally confronts reality.

In Acts 21–26, Paul stands before a series of powerful authorities, and something similar unfolds, only in reverse. Paul is the prisoner, but he is not the one who needs saving. The people questioning him are. Every courtroom becomes a pulpit. Every accusation becomes an opportunity to preach the gospel. The judges think they are examining Paul, but Paul is the one offering them the truth that could change their lives.

Paul appears before the Jewish mob in Jerusalem, the Sanhedrin, the Roman governor Felix, the governor Festus, and finally King Agrippa. Five audiences. Five defenses. And in every one of them, Paul says the same thing: Jesus is alive. He appeared to me. And this changes everything.

WALKING INTO THE STORM

Paul knew what was waiting for him. On his way to Jerusalem, prophets in city after city warned him. In Tyre, disciples urged him not to go (21:4). In Caesarea, a prophet named Agabus took Paul's belt, tied his own hands and feet with it, and said, "The Holy Spirit says: 'In this way the Jewish leaders in Jerusalem will bind the owner of this belt and will hand him over to the Gentiles'" (21:11). The Christians around Paul wept and begged him to stay away.

Paul's answer was unflinching: "Why are you weeping and breaking my heart? I am ready not only to be bound, but also to die in Jerusalem for the name of the Lord Jesus" (21:13).

His friends finally stopped arguing. "The Lord's will be done," they said (21:14).

Paul walked into Jerusalem with his eyes wide open. He knew the cost. He went anyway.

SEIZED IN THE TEMPLE

When Paul arrived, the Jerusalem elders warned him that thousands of Jewish believers were zealous for the law and had heard rumors that Paul was teaching Jews to abandon Moses. To show his respect for the law, Paul agreed to join four men in a purification ritual at the temple (21:23–26).

It didn't matter. Jews from the province of Asia spotted Paul in the temple courts, recognized him, and started a riot. "Men of Israel, help us!" they screamed. "This is the man who teaches everyone everywhere against our people and our law and this place. And besides, he has brought Greeks into the temple and defiled this holy place" (21:28). The second charge was false. They had seen Paul in the city with a Gentile friend and assumed he had brought him into the restricted area.

The whole city was stirred up. The mob dragged Paul out of the temple and began beating him. He would have been killed if the Roman commander had not arrived with soldiers and taken him into custody (21:31–33). As the soldiers carried Paul up the steps of the barracks, the crowd surged behind them, shouting, "Get rid of him!" (21:36).

From the top of those steps, Paul asked permission to speak.

DEFENSE ONE: THE CROWD

Standing above the mob that had just tried to kill him, Paul addressed them in their own language. The crowd fell silent.

He told them his story. He was a Jew, born in Tarsus, educated in Jerusalem under the great teacher Gamaliel, zealous for God, and a former persecutor of the Way. He described the light on the Damascus road, the voice of Jesus, his blindness, and how a devout man named Ananias came to him and said, "Get up, be baptized and wash your sins away, calling on his name" (22:16).

The crowd listened until Paul mentioned the word that set them off: Gentiles. When he said that the Lord had told him, "Go; I will send you far away to the Gentiles" (22:21), the mob erupted. They tore their clothes and threw dust in the air, screaming for his death.

The commander ordered Paul brought inside and prepared to have him flogged to find out why the crowd was so furious. But Paul asked the centurion standing nearby, "Is it legal for you to flog a Roman citizen who hasn't even been found guilty?" (22:25). The centurion froze. The commander came immediately. He had purchased his Roman citizenship at a high price. Paul had been born with it (22:28).

The flogging was cancelled. Paul would get a proper hearing.

DEFENSE TWO: THE SANHEDRIN

The next day, the commander brought Paul before the Sanhedrin. Paul looked straight at the council and said, "My brothers, I have fulfilled my duty to God in all good conscience to this day" (23:1). The high priest Ananias ordered someone to strike him on the mouth.

Paul fired back: "God will strike you, you whitewashed wall! You sit there to judge me according to the law, yet you yourself violate the law by commanding that I be struck!" (23:3).

Then Paul used his knowledge of the council's divisions to his advantage. Knowing that the Sadducees denied the resurrection while the Pharisees affirmed it, he declared, "I stand on trial because of the hope of the resurrection of the dead" (23:6). The room immediately split. The Pharisees defended him. The Sadducees attacked him. The argument became so violent that the commander had to send soldiers to pull Paul out before he was torn apart.

That night, alone in the barracks, Paul received the visit he needed most. The Lord stood near him and said, "Take courage! As you have testified about me in Jerusalem, so you must also testify in Rome" (23:11).

Rome. The mission was not over. It was being redirected.

A PLOT AND AN ESCAPE

The next morning, more than forty men took an oath that they would not eat or drink until they had killed Paul. They convinced the chief priests to request another hearing, planning to ambush Paul on the way.

But Paul's nephew, a young man whose name Luke never tells us, heard about the plot. He reported it to Paul, who sent him to the Roman commander. The commander believed the boy, assembled an escort of two hundred soldiers, seventy horsemen, and two hundred spearmen, and transferred Paul to Caesarea under cover of night (23:23–24). The prisoner was moved like a king under guard. Paul was out of Jerusalem, alive, and on his way toward Rome, exactly as the Lord had promised.

DEFENSE THREE: GOVERNOR FELIX

In Caesarea, Paul stood trial before the Roman governor Felix. The Jewish leaders hired a professional lawyer named Tertullus, who accused Paul of being "a troublemaker, stirring up riots among the Jews all over the world" and "a ringleader of the Nazarene sect" who tried to desecrate the temple (24:5–6).

Paul's defense was calm and factual. He had gone to Jerusalem to worship, not to start a riot. No one had found him arguing with anyone in the temple or stirring up a crowd in the synagogues. He did admit one thing: "I worship the God of our ancestors as a follower of the Way, which they call a sect. I believe everything that is in agreement with the Law and that is written in the Prophets, and I have the same hope in God as these men themselves have, that there will be a resurrection of both the righteous and the wicked" (24:14-15).

Felix knew more about the Way than most Roman officials. He adjourned the case but kept Paul in custody. Over the following days, Felix sent for Paul privately and listened to him speak about faith in Christ Jesus. But when Paul talked about righteousness, self-control, and the coming judgment, Felix grew afraid. "That's enough for now," he said. "When I find it convenient, I will send for you" (24:25).

That convenient time never came. Felix left Paul in prison for two years, hoping Paul would offer him a bribe. He never did.

DEFENSE FOUR: GOVERNOR FESTUS

When Festus replaced Felix as governor, the Jewish leaders immediately asked him to transfer Paul back to Jerusalem, planning another ambush along the way. Festus refused but held a new hearing in Caesarea. The accusations were the same. Paul's defense was the same: "I have done nothing wrong against the Jewish law or against the temple or against Caesar" (25:8).

Festus, wanting to do the Jews a favor, asked Paul if he was willing to go to Jerusalem for trial. Paul had had enough. "I am now standing before Caesar's court, where I ought to be tried," he said. "If I am guilty of doing anything deserving death, I do not refuse to die. But if the charges brought against me by these Jews are not true, no one has the right to hand me over to them. I appeal to Caesar!" (25:10–11).

Those three words changed everything. As a Roman citizen, Paul had the right to have his case heard by the emperor himself. Festus consulted his advisors and then answered, "You have appealed to Caesar. To Caesar you will go!" (25:12).

The road to Rome was now officially open.

DEFENSE FIVE: KING AGRIPPA

Before Paul could be sent to Rome, King Agrippa II arrived in Caesarea with his sister Bernice to pay their respects to the new governor. Festus told Agrippa about Paul's case, and Agrippa asked to hear the man himself.

The next day, Agrippa and Bernice entered the audience hall with great pomp, accompanied by high-ranking military officers and the leading men of the city. Paul was brought in, a prisoner standing before a king.

Paul gave his most complete and personal defense. He spoke of his upbringing as a strict Pharisee, his persecution of the church, and then, for the third time in Acts, he told the story of the Damascus road: the blinding light, the voice of Jesus, the commission to carry the gospel to Jews and Gentiles alike. He told Agrippa that Jesus had appeared to him and said, "I am sending you to open their eyes and turn them from darkness to light, and from the power of Satan to God, so that they may receive forgiveness of sins and a place among those who are sanctified by faith in me" (26:17–18).

Paul had not been disobedient to the heavenly vision, he said. He had been doing exactly what Jesus told him to do. And everything he preached was nothing more than what Moses and the prophets had predicted: "that the Messiah would suffer and, as the first to rise from the dead, would bring the message of light to his own people and to the Gentiles" (26:22–23).

At this point, Festus interrupted. "You are out of your mind, Paul!" he shouted. "Your great learning is driving you insane!" (26:24).

Paul answered calmly, "I am not insane, most excellent Festus. What I am saying is true and reasonable. The king is familiar with these things. I am convinced that none of this has escaped his notice, because it was not done in a corner" (26:25–26). Then he turned to Agrippa directly: "King Agrippa, do you believe the prophets? I know you do" (26:27).

Agrippa's reply has echoed through the centuries: "Do you think that in such a short time you can persuade me to be a Christian?" (26:28).

Paul's answer is one of the most beautiful lines in Scripture: "Short time or long, I pray to God that not only you but all who are listening to me today may become what I am, except for these chains" (26:29).

The hearing ended. Agrippa and Festus withdrew and agreed: "This man is not doing anything that deserves death or imprisonment." Agrippa said to Festus, "This man could have been set free if he had not appealed to Caesar" (26:31–32).

But Paul had appealed. And Rome was waiting.

WHAT THIS MEANS FOR US

First, obedience sometimes means walking toward the hard thing, not away from it. Paul's friends begged him not to go to Jerusalem. He went because the Spirit compelled him and the mission required it. Faithfulness to God does not always lead away from danger. Sometimes it leads straight into it.

Second, every platform is a pulpit. Paul was dragged from one courtroom to another, but he never treated his trials as mere legal proceedings. Every defense was a sermon. Every audience was a mission field. If you belong to Jesus, no situation is wasted. Even the hardest circumstances can become opportunities to speak the truth.

Third, people respond to the gospel in different ways. The mob wanted Paul dead. Felix was intrigued but procrastinated. Festus thought Paul was insane. Agrippa was almost persuaded but held back. The same message, heard by different hearts, produced completely different responses. You cannot control how people react to the truth. You can only make sure you tell it faithfully.

Fourth, God's plans cannot be derailed. Forty men swore an oath to kill Paul. Two governors tried to use him as a political pawn. The Jewish leaders hounded him at every turn. And yet Paul ended up exactly where Jesus said he would: on his way to Rome. When God says, "You must testify," no conspiracy, no courtroom, and no prison can prevent it.

TALKING POINTS

1. **Paul knew that prison and hardship were waiting for him in Jerusalem, but he went anyway. His friends thought**

he was being reckless, but Paul believed he was being obedient. What made the difference? How can you tell when a difficult decision is an act of faith rather than an act of carelessness?

2. **Paul told his story, including his conversion on the Damascus road, three times in Acts.** Why do you think personal testimony is such a powerful tool for sharing the gospel? What parts of your own story could you share with others?

3. **Felix was afraid when Paul talked about righteousness, self-control, and the judgment to come.** Why do you think those subjects made him uncomfortable? Are there parts of the gospel that make people today uncomfortable for the same reasons?

4. **Agrippa said, "Do you think that in such a short time you can persuade me to be a Christian?"** What do you think held him back? What keeps people today from fully responding to the gospel even when they know it is true?

5. **Paul said he wished everyone listening could become what he was, "except for these chains."** What does it tell you about Paul that he could say this while standing in a courtroom as a prisoner? How can someone have that kind of joy and confidence even in a terrible situation?

Paul had stood before mobs, councils, governors, and a king. He had been beaten, bound, and locked away for more than two years. He had been declared innocent three times over, and yet he was still in chains.

But the Lord had spoken. Rome was the destination. And the most dangerous journey of Paul's life was about to begin.

Turn the page.

12

UNHINDERED

The Black Stallion begins on a ship. A young boy named Alec Ramsey is aboard a steamer crossing the ocean when everything goes wrong. A storm hammers the vessel. The ship breaks apart and sinks. Alec is thrown into the churning water with nothing to hold onto except the rope of a wild black stallion he had befriended during the voyage. The horse pulls him through the waves, and when the sun rises, they wash up together on a deserted island.

They have lost everything. The ship, the passengers, the plan. But on that island, in the wreckage of a disaster that should have killed them both, something new begins. The boy and the horse form a bond that will carry them further than either could have gone alone.

The book of Acts sort of ends with a shipwreck too.

Paul, chained and under guard, boards a ship bound for Rome. He has been promised by the risen Jesus that he will testify before Caesar. But between the promise and the destination lies the worst storm Luke has ever described, a ship torn to pieces in the open sea, and an island nobody planned to visit. Everything looks like it's falling apart.

But the word of God cannot sink. And neither can the man carrying it.

SAILING INTO DANGER

Paul boarded the ship as a prisoner in the custody of a Roman centurion named Julius. Luke and a believer named Aristarchus traveled with him. They sailed along the coast, stopping at Sidon, where Julius kindly allowed Paul to visit friends and receive care (27:3). From there they sailed under the shelter of Cyprus because the winds were against them.

Progress was slow and difficult. By the time they reached a place called Fair Havens on the island of Crete, the sailing season was nearly over. Paul warned the centurion and the ship's officers: "Men, I can see that our voyage is going to be disastrous and bring great loss to ship and cargo, and to our own lives also" (27:10).

They didn't listen. The harbor at Fair Havens was not a good place to spend the winter, so the majority decided to push on to a better port further down the coast. It seemed like a reasonable decision.

It nearly killed them all.

FOURTEEN DAYS OF DARKNESS

A gentle south wind tricked them into thinking conditions were safe. They weighed anchor and hugged the coastline. But almost immediately, a hurricane-force wind called a northeaster slammed into the ship. The crew couldn't hold their course. They were driven out into the open sea, battered by waves, with no way to steer.

For days, the storm did not let up. The crew threw the cargo overboard. Then they threw the ship's tackle overboard. When neither sun nor stars appeared for many days, and the storm continued raging, Luke says that "we finally gave up all hope of being saved" (27:20).

All hope gone. Two hundred and seventy-six people on a ship in the middle of the Mediterranean, and every one of them believed they were going to die.

Then Paul stood up.

"Men, you should have taken my advice not to sail from Crete," he said, and you can almost hear the exhaustion in his voice. "But now I urge you to keep up your courage, because not one of you will be lost; only the ship will be destroyed" (27:21–22).

How could he possibly know that?

"Last night an angel of the God to whom I belong and whom I serve stood beside me and said, 'Do not be afraid, Paul. You must stand trial before Caesar; and God has graciously given you the lives of all who sail with you.' So keep up your courage, men, for I have faith in God that it will happen just as he told me" (27:23–25).

In the darkest moment of the journey, a prisoner became the leader. Paul had no rank on that ship. He had no authority over the crew. But he had something none of them had: a word from God. And that was enough.

On the fourteenth night, the sailors sensed they were approaching land. They took soundings and found the water was getting shallower. Fearing they would crash on rocks in the darkness, they dropped four anchors from the stern and prayed for daylight.

When dawn finally came, they spotted a sandy bay. They cut the anchors, hoisted the foresail, and headed for the beach. The ship struck a sandbar and stuck fast. The bow jammed in and would not move, and the stern was being broken apart by the pounding surf.

The soldiers planned to kill the prisoners to prevent any of them from swimming away and escaping. But Julius the centurion wanted to spare Paul's life, so he stopped them. He ordered everyone who could swim to jump overboard first and the rest to grab planks or pieces of the ship and float to shore.

Everyone reached land safely. Not a single life was lost. Just as the angel had promised.

THE ISLAND

They discovered they were on the island of Malta. The islanders showed them unusual kindness, building a fire and welcoming the drenched, shivering survivors (28:2).

As Paul gathered a bundle of sticks and placed them on the fire, a viper, driven out by the heat, fastened itself onto his hand. The islanders saw the snake hanging from his arm and said to each other, "This man must be a murderer; for though he escaped from the sea, the goddess Justice has not allowed him to live" (28:4).

Paul shook the snake off into the fire and suffered no harm. The people watched, waiting for him to swell up or suddenly fall dead. When nothing happened, they changed their minds and decided he must be a god (28:6).

Luke records these reactions without commentary, but the pattern should look familiar by now. In Lystra, the crowd thought Paul was a god when he healed a lame man, then stoned him the same day. Here the pattern is reversed: they assumed he was a condemned criminal, then decided he was divine. Both responses were wrong. Paul was neither a criminal nor a god. He was a servant of the living God, protected for a purpose.

The chief official of the island, a man named Publius, welcomed Paul and his companions into his home. Publius' father was sick with fever and dysentery. Paul went in, prayed, placed his hands on the man, and healed him. After that, the rest of the sick on the island came and were cured (28:8–9). The islanders honored Paul and his companions and supplied them with everything they needed when they set sail again.

Even on an unplanned island, in the aftermath of a disaster, the gospel did its work. Paul healed. Paul served. And the name of Jesus was honored among people who had never heard it before.

ROME AT LAST

After three months on Malta, they set sail on another ship and finally reached Italy. When they landed at Puteoli, they found believers already there and stayed with them for seven days. Word traveled ahead, and as Paul approached Rome, Christians from the city came out to meet him along the road, some traveling as far as forty miles from the capital to greet him. When Paul saw them, Luke tells us, "he thanked God and was encouraged" (28:15).

Think about what this moment meant. Paul had been dreaming of Rome for years. He had written to the Roman church from Corinth. He had told the Ephesian elders he would never see them again because the Spirit was driving him toward this city. Jesus himself had stood beside him in a barracks in Jerusalem and said, "You must testify in Rome."

Now he was here. In chains, yes. But here.

Paul was allowed to live by himself in Rome, with a soldier to guard him (28:16). He wasted no time. Three days after arriving, he invited the local Jewish leaders to his rented house and explained his situation. He told them he had done nothing against the Jewish people or the customs of their ancestors. He had been handed over to the Romans, who found no basis for a death sentence. He had been forced to appeal to Caesar, not because he had any charge to bring against his own nation, but because he had no other choice. "It is because of the hope of Israel," he told them, "that I am bound with this chain" (28:20).

The hope of Israel. That phrase captures everything Paul had been saying in every courtroom and before every audience since his arrest. He was not preaching a foreign religion. He was proclaiming the fulfillment of Israel's oldest and deepest hope: that God would raise the dead, that the Messiah would come, and that through him the light of salvation would reach the ends of the earth.

The Jewish leaders in Rome agreed to hear more. On a set day, they came in large numbers to Paul's lodging. From morning till evening, Paul explained and declared the kingdom of God, trying to persuade them about Jesus from the Law of Moses and from the Prophets (28:23).

Some were convinced. Others refused to believe. As they left, disagreeing among themselves, Paul spoke one last word. He quoted the prophet Isaiah's warning about people who hear but never understand, who look but never see, whose hearts have grown calloused (28:26–27). Then he said, "Therefore I want you to know that God's salvation has been sent to the Gentiles, and they will listen!" (28:28).

THE LAST WORD

The final two verses of Acts are among the most discussed in all of the New Testament. "For two whole years Paul stayed there in his own rented house and welcomed all who came to see him. He proclaimed the kingdom of God and taught about the Lord Jesus Christ, with all boldness and without hindrance" (28:30–31).

That's it. That's how the book ends.

No verdict from Caesar. No release. No execution. No final scene of Paul walking free or dying for his faith. Just a man in a rented room, chained to a soldier, preaching the kingdom of God to everyone who walked through the door.

And the very last word Luke wrote, the word he chose to close the entire book, is "without hindrance."

Of all the ways Luke could have ended this story, he chose that word. After riots and shipwrecks, after beatings and trials, after two years in a Caesarean prison and a harrowing voyage across the sea, the gospel arrived in Rome and was being preached openly, boldly, and without anyone stopping it.

The authorities couldn't stop it. The storms couldn't stop it. The chains couldn't stop it. The Jewish leaders who rejected it couldn't stop it. Caesar himself, the most powerful man on earth, could not stop the message of a crucified and risen carpenter from Nazareth from being proclaimed in the heart of his own capital city.

WHAT THIS MEANS FOR US

First, God keeps his promises, even when the road to fulfillment is terrifying. Jesus told Paul he would testify in Rome. He never said the trip would be easy. Between the promise and its fulfillment lay a hurricane, a shipwreck, a snakebite, and years of imprisonment. But Paul arrived exactly where God said he would. When God makes a promise, the storms along the way do not cancel it. They are part of the route.

Second, your circumstances do not determine your usefulness. Paul was a prisoner chained to a Roman soldier, living in a rented room. By the world's standards, his ministry was over. But from that room he preached the kingdom of God to everyone who came through the door, and he wrote letters that would shape the faith of billions of people for thousands of years. God does not need you to be free, comfortable, or powerful to use you. He needs you to be faithful wherever you are.

Third, the gospel speaks to every kind of person. In these two chapters alone, Paul interacted with a Roman centurion, a ship full of terrified sailors, the islanders of Malta, a local chief and his sick father, Jewish leaders in Rome, and countless others. He adapted to each situation without ever changing the message. The truth about Jesus is relevant to every culture, every class, and every corner of the world. It always has been.

Fourth, nothing can ultimately stop the word of God. That is the message of the entire book of Acts, and it is the message of these final verses. Persecution scattered the church and the gospel spread. Prison silenced Paul's public ministry and he preached from a rented room. A ship sank and Paul healed the sick on an island nobody had planned to visit. At every point where it looked like the mission was finished, God opened another door. The word of the Lord is unhindered, and it always will be.

TALKING POINTS

1. **Paul warned the ship's crew not to sail, but they ignored him and the voyage nearly ended in disaster.** When has someone given you wise advice that you didn't follow? What happened? How do you learn to recognize wisdom when it's offered?

2. **In the middle of the storm, Paul stood up and told 276 terrified people that an angel had promised their safety.** What gave Paul the confidence to speak hope into a hopeless situation? Where does that kind of courage come from?

3. **On Malta, the islanders first thought Paul was a murderer, then a god. Neither was true.** Why are people so quick to put others into extreme categories? How should Christians respond when they are misunderstood?

4. **Acts ends with Paul under house arrest, still preaching.** Why do you think Luke chose to end the book this way instead of telling us what happened to Paul? What does this unfinished ending suggest about the mission of the church?

5. **The last word of Acts is "unhindered."** Looking back over the whole book, what were the biggest obstacles the gospel faced? How did God overcome each one? What does this

tell you about whether anything can ultimately stop the message of Jesus?

When the book of Acts began, a small group of frightened disciples stood on a hillside near Jerusalem, watching Jesus disappear into a cloud. They had no money, no power, and no plan except the one he had given them: wait for the Spirit, and then be my witnesses to the ends of the earth.

By the time the book ends, those witnesses have carried the gospel from a rented room in Jerusalem to the capital of the Roman Empire. The message has crossed seas, climbed mountains, survived prisons, outlasted empires, and reached people that no one in that first gathering on the hillside could have imagined.

And the story is not over.

Luke set down his pen, but the mission kept going. The same Spirit who filled the apostles at Pentecost, who opened Lydia's heart in Philippi, who shook the walls of a prison at midnight, who stood beside Paul on a sinking ship and said "Do not be afraid," is still at work today. The book of Acts has no final chapter because the final chapter has not been written yet. It is being written right now, in every city and village and school and home where someone opens their mouth and tells the truth about Jesus.

The gospel is still unhindered.

And it always will be.